INTRODUCTION

Welcome to *Baritone Ukulele Aerobics*: your one-stop-shop for building formidable baritone uke chops. If you've grown tired of strumming your open chords (though there's certainly nothing wrong with that!) and desire to spice up your playing with a bit of flair or variety, this book will be your guide. Today's uke is not your father's uke. Just check out Jake Shimabukuro, James Hill, or Roy Smeck (OK, so he did play your father's uke, but not enough people know about him, which is a shame!) to hear what's capable on this instrument. However, all those players specialize on the smaller ukes (*soprano* or *concert*). The baritone feels a bit different—not to mention the tuning is different (see Tuning section)—hence the creation of this book. (My first book on the subject, *Ukulele Aerobics*, also published by Hal Leonard, is designed for the soprano or concert uke.)

It may be a bit daunting upon first watching the virtuosos listed above—especially if you've only strummed a few open chords thus far in your uke studies—but it's important to remember that Rome wasn't built in a day. Even those players started off as beginners at some point. In *Baritone Ukulele Aerobics*, we take a structured approach that focuses on a different technique or musical concept each day of the week. If you stick to the program (but don't beat yourself up if you miss a day or two!), you can't help but vastly improve your skills. I've tried my best to make these exercises and examples musically interesting and inspiring while still teaching you solid concepts that you can apply in future uke arrangements for many years to come. To help keep things fresh, we'll cover different styles; when you've got a 40-week practice program on your calendar, the last thing you want is monotony.

The material of this book is fairly comprehensive, spanning from beginner-level material at the front to advanced topics by the end. If you're an absolute beginner on the instrument, you may want to work through a complete beginner method before tackling this program, as it does assume a basic familiarity with the instrument. For more experienced players, the earlier weeks may seem to be nothing but a review, but I encourage you to work through them just in case you come across something that's new. And who couldn't use a bit of review, anyway?

Regardless of your skill level, you can be sure that you'll improve by leaps and bounds if you work through the entire book. I thoroughly enjoyed writing this book and recording the accompanying audio, and I hope you enjoy it too. Best of luck in your musical journey!

T0087269

HOW TO USE THIS BOOK

Baritone Ukulele Aerobics is arranged in weekly practice units, with each day focusing on a different concept, to ensure that all facets of technique are given equal attention. For the most part, the material progresses in difficulty throughout the book, although there may be a few slight digressions along the way due to some overlapping of various concepts and techniques. Here's an overview of the technical breakdown day-by-day:

Monday – Chord Vocabulary: This is all about developing your chord vocabulary. The more chords you know, the better equipped you are and the more versatile you'll be in any situation. We'll start extremely basic, but by the end, you'll be learning altered dominants and more! Most chords are shown two ways: as an open form (containing one or more open strings) and a moveable form (containing no open strings). The moveable forms can be slid anywhere on the neck to play from different roots, and this will often be done in several workouts from the same week.

Tuesday – Strumming: This day will concentrate on developing solid strumming skills. The examples progress from basic and straightforward to highly syncopated and cover everything in between, including various muted strum effects and other specific technical challenges.

Wednesday – Fingerstyle: You'll expand your horizons by leaps and bounds by adding the fingerstyle technique to your bag of tricks.

Thursday – Scale Exercises: This day specifically concentrates on single-note playing. Both hands will receive a workout on this one.

Friday – Legato: Though the ukulele doesn't have much sustain, the legato technique is still incredibly useful in both scalar and chordal playing. This day works on all aspects and is certain to build significant strength in your fretting hand.

Saturday – Licks & Riffs: This is the fun day each week. We get to apply your newly acquired skills to licks or riffs in various styles throughout.

Sunday – Miscellaneous: This day will be pretty fun as well. It's geared toward studying various specific techniques or concepts that don't neatly fit into the five categories covered in Monday–Friday. Examples include tremolo, double stops, vibrato, and so forth.

Each example in this book is recorded on the accompanying audio at a moderate tempo. If it's too fast at first, set a metronome at a tempo that you can handle and gradually increase the speed until you're able to play along flawlessly. But don't feel obligated to stop there! Continue raising the tempo if you choose to challenge yourself.

A note on terminology: When I say "low" and "high" with regards to notes or strings on the ukulele, I'm almost always referring to pitch and not physical location. So the *lowest* string is the thickest (string 4, D); the *highest* string is the thinnest (string 1, E).

Although the book is laid out in a specific day-by-day approach, feel free to tailor it to your needs. If you're not able to practice every day of the week, you can break each week's material up into two weeks, for example. Or if, after working through a week, you don't feel you've mastered the material, feel free to repeat it. The point is to keep progressing once you've got the material under your fingers. Slow and steady wins the race in this regard; it's definitely better to practice for 20 minutes every day than to cram four hours in on a Sunday.

Audio Access Included

BARITONE UKULELE
AEROBICS

BY CHAD JOHNSON

To access audio visit:
www.halleonard.com/mylibrary

Enter Code
2858-0266-4434-8864

Cover Illustration by Birck Cox

ISBN 978-1-4950-7575-9

HAL•LEONARD®

7777 W. BLUEMOUND RD. P.O. BOX 13819 MILWAUKEE, WI 53213

In Australia Contact:
Hal Leonard Australia Pty. Ltd.
4 Lentara Court
Cheltenham, Victoria, 3192 Australia
Email: ausadmin@halleonard.com.au

Visit Hal Leonard Online at
www.halleonard.com

CONTENTS

BARITONE UKULELE TUNING

Whereas the soprano (standard) and concert ukuleles generally use the reentrant tuning of G–C–E–A (also known as C6 tuning or the "My Dog Has Fleas" tuning), the strings of a baritone ukulele are tuned (low pitch to high) D–G–B–E. Coincidentally, these are the same exact pitches as the top four strings on a guitar, which makes it very easy for a player to transition from one to the other. If you don't have a tuner, you can use the following audio track to get the pitches.

Tuning Notes

DEDICATION & ACKNOWLEDGMENTS

This book is dedicated to my loving family: my wife Allison, son Lennon, and daughter Leherie. I'm so incredibly grateful for every day with each of you.

Thanks for all the wonderful efforts from the people at Hal Leonard Corporation. It's always an honor to work with them.

I'd also like to acknowledge the tremendous talents of Jake Shimabukuro and James Hill, in particular, both of whom continue to push the ukulele into new and inspiring areas of musical expression.

MON

Chord Vocabulary: These are the five most common major chords you'll come across on the baritone uke: G, E, D, C, and A. They're all **open chords**, meaning they include at least one open string.

G   E   D   C   A

TUE

Strumming: We'll start very basic, strumming each of the five chords in half notes (two beat counts for each strum). Use **downstrokes** (toward the floor) for each of these chords, brushing through the strings with your thumb. (The ⊓ symbol indicates a downstroke.) Try counting along with the beat ("1, 2, 3, 4") as you strum. The focus here is on three things: 1) cleanly fretting each chord, 2) achieving a balanced strum sound with each string ringing out, and 3) playing **in time** (i.e., not rushing or dragging).

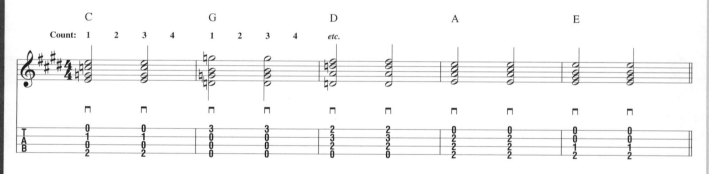

WED

Fingerstyle: In fingerstyle, you'll be using your thumb and fingers to pluck the strings. Some people use their thumb and index only; others use the thumb, index, and middle; and others incorporate the ring finger as well. The pinky is rarely used in this context. (With only four strings, who needs it?) We'll start off by simply playing **arpeggios** (broken chords) through the same progression we saw on Tuesday. Start by planting your thumb on string 4, index on string 3, middle on string 2, and ring on string 1. Strive for an even volume throughout. The plucking-hand fingers are indicated throughout as follows: t = thumb, i = index, m = middle, and r = ring.

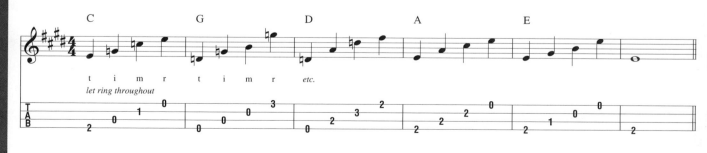

THU

Scale Exercise: We'll start with a simple G major scale that's played on the top three strings in steady quarter notes (one note per beat). Pluck the notes with either your thumb or index finger. Regarding your fret hand, remain in first position throughout. This means that your first finger is placed at fret 1 and will play all notes at that fret. Your second finger plays the notes on fret 2, your third plays the notes on fret 3, etc.

FRI

Legato: The musical term **legato** means "smooth and connected." On the ukulele, we usually accomplish this with two specific techniques: **hammer-ons** and **pull-offs**. These are indicated in the music with a curved line, called a **slur**, connecting the notes. To perform these hammer-ons (measures 1–2), pluck the open string and then forcefully "hammer" your fret-hand finger down onto the string at fret 2 (or 3) as indicated. For the pull-offs (measures 3–4), pluck the fretted note and then pull that fret-hand finger down (toward the floor) and off the string to sound the open string. You're essentially using that fret-hand finger to pluck the open string. Strive for even tempo and volume throughout.

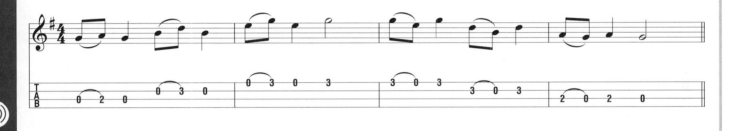

SAT

Licks & Riffs: This is the fun day, when we get to apply one or more of the techniques to a **lick** or a **riff**—a short musical phrase. This is a nice little phrase in G that combines several elements we've looked at so far: first position, legato, the G major scale, and C and G chords. In case you don't know, "N.C." stands for "no chord."

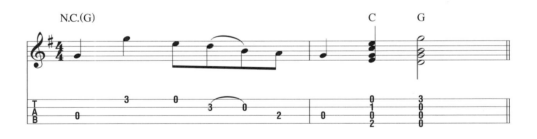

SUN

Miscellaneous: Let's take a look at how easy it is to create different chords by moving only one note in a certain chord. We'll start with G major here and see what happens when we simply move the top note down one fret at a time. You'll see this idea in many songs as a way to spice things up a bit. (Note that the fourth chord could be called G6 or Em7.)

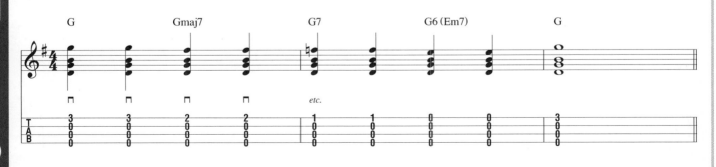

MON

Chord Vocabulary: Let's continue our chord study by looking at some common open chords in the key of G— aside from the G, C, and D chords you already learned in Week 1. We see our first minor chords (Em and Am), a dominant 7th chord (D7), and the Gmaj7 that we first encountered on Sunday of Week 1, where we created different chords by moving the top note of the G chord down. There's also an alternate voicing of the C chord, which has the note G on top. (The term **voicing** refers to the vertical arrangement of the different notes in a chord. As we'll see throughout the book, there are many different ways to play the same chord on the baritone uke.)

Em   Am   D7   Gmaj7   C

TUE

Strumming: This week we're mixing quarter notes (one strum per beat) and half notes (one strum every two beats) with a nice chord progression in G major. Again, brush down with your thumb to strum. You'll have less time to prepare for some of the chords because of the quarter notes, but one of the other main focuses here is the rhythm. Make sure you're not rushing through the half notes; give them their full two-beat duration. Also notice the alternate C chord voicing in measure 3, demonstrating how we can create little melodies within the chords by using different voicings.

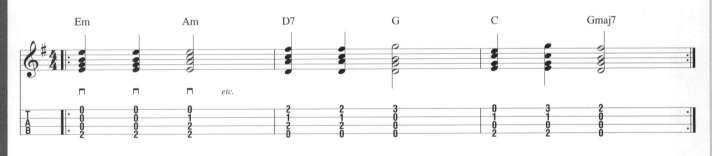

WED

Fingerstyle: This week we'll add eighth notes (two plucks per beat) to the mix to create a flowing arpeggio pattern through a G major progression. Again, be sure to maintain a steady tempo throughout; this is critical to becoming a competent accompanist on the instrument. Notice also that the pattern diverges slightly in measure 4, where we descend back through the strings of the D7 chord. The wavy line next to the G chord in measure 5 indicates that you should smoothly brush through the strings (with your thumb in this case). Think of it as kind of a deliberate, smooth strum. Listen to the audio to hear how it sounds.

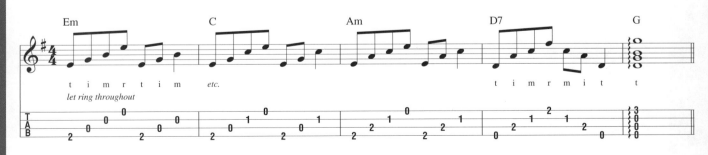

THU

Scale Exercise: We'll use the same G major scale from Week 1, but this time we're combining eighth and quarter notes. The tempo isn't too quick, so it shouldn't be too technically difficult. You can still pluck each note with your thumb (or index finger), but be sure to maintain steady time. Tap your foot on the beat as you play; this helps to solidify your tempo.

FRI

Legato: We'll use the same G major pentatonic scale form from last week here, but we'll increase the difficulty by jumping back and forth between the strings more. We're also including the D string this time. Each one-bar hammer-on phrase is answered by a similar one using pull-offs.

SAT

Licks & Riffs: Here's a nice little lick, again in G major, similar to last week but with a few more eighth notes and a different rhythm. This lick uses what's called a **swing feel** (or **shuffle feel**), which is indicated by the rhythmic symbol with the equals sign. This means that the eighth notes are played with a "lopsided" feel, in which the first one of each beat lasts longer than the second. It's easier to hear it than it is to explain it, so listen to the audio. You'll no doubt recognize it. Also notice the dot below the final G chord. This is called a **staccato** marking, and it indicates that a chord (or note) should be played in a clipped, abrupt manner. It's kind of the opposite of legato (in feel—not technique). Strum through the chord quickly and then mute the strings by laying the side of your strumming hand down on them to stop them from ringing out.

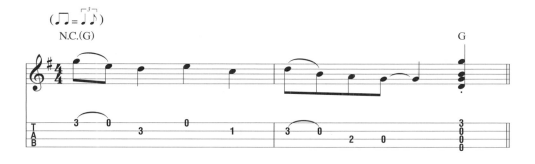

SUN

Miscellaneous: We'll do a variation on last week's idea here involving a new technique. After strumming through each chord with your thumb, use an upstroke with your index finger to pluck the note on string 1. The motion should be smooth and connected, with the thumb moving down through the strings and the index finger plucking the top string as the thumb moves back into position for the next strum. This is a nice way to bring out a particular note in a strumming pattern.

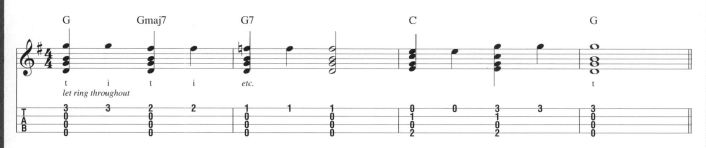

WEEK 3

MON

Chord Vocabulary: Let's continue learning more open chords in the key of G. We've seen major, minor, and 7th chords so far. Here we also have a G5, or a G power chord. A **power chord** contains only the root and 5th of the chord. We can also play a D5 by simply muting the top string of a D chord. To do this, just allow the pad of your second or third finger (whichever you're using for string 2) to touch string 1. Then we have three **suspended chords**—sus4 in this case. In these chords, the 3rd degree has been replaced with the 4th.

TUE

Strumming: Here we're putting our new sus4 chords to work in a strumming pattern that introduces eighth notes. For this pattern, you'll be alternating downstrokes and upstrokes, indicated in the music by the symbol ⊓ for down and V for up. You can do the upstroke with the thumb, but also try it with the index finger curled into somewhat of a hook shape. Rather than moving the forearm down and up, the motion should come from twisting the wrist—almost as if you were opening a door knob. When counting eighth notes, use "and" in between the beats: "1 & 2 & 3 & 4 &," etc.

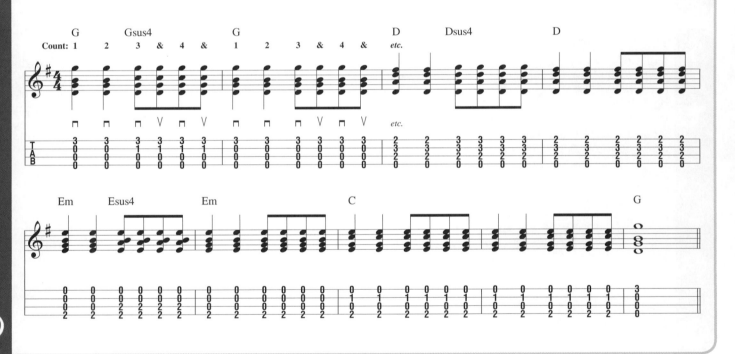

WED

Fingerstyle: This is another eighth-note pattern, but this one is adapted a bit from a guitar approach. We're using our index and middle fingers for strings 2 and 1, respectively, but the thumb is alternating between strings 4 and 3. You could still play this pattern using the thumb and three fingers, but it's a bit easier to keep a steady sense of time with your thumb hitting the downbeats like this.

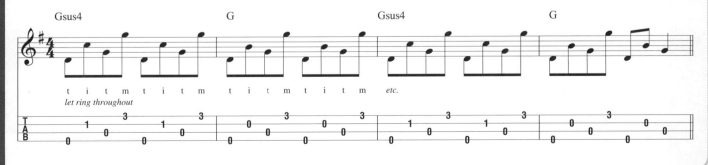

THU

Scale Exercise: This is our first scale sequence, using the G major scale. A **sequence** is basically a pattern of notes that repeats at different pitch levels. Just as we can create a numerical sequence, such as 1-3-2-4-3-5-4-6, etc., we can do the same with the notes of a scale. This exercise is known as a 3rds sequence, because each note is followed by another that's three note names away: G down to E, F# down to D, etc. You can try plucking this several ways: using the thumb only, alternating your index and middle fingers, or alternating your thumb and index (or middle) finger. Try them all out to see what feels or sounds best to you. Starting on beat 3 of measure 2, you can either remain in first position and use your middle finger and pinky for frets 2 and 4, respectively, or you can shift to second position and use your index and ring fingers.

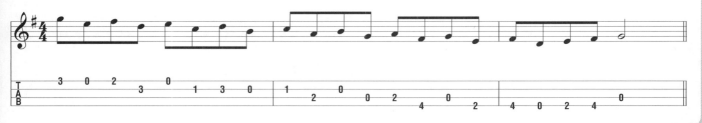

FRI

Legato: Although we're only working with pull-offs here, we're increasing the difficulty by stringing two of them together in a row. To do this, we'll descend through the G major scale in open position, plucking only once on each string. The most difficult part of this exercise is getting both pull-offs to sound clearly. In order to do this, you really need to be pulling off in a downward motion (toward the floor) while using a fair amount of pressure so the string will vibrate clearly.

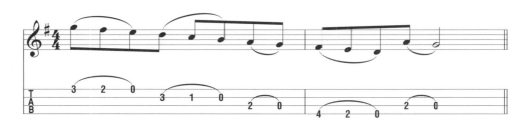

SAT

Licks & Riffs: Here's a bluesy-sounding riff in G that mixes **double stops** (two notes played simultaneously) with a pull-off and hammer-on at fret 3. Be sure to notice the staccato marking on the C note at fret 1, string 2. This really helps make the riff pop.

SUN

Miscellaneous: Let's work a bit more with double stops in the key of G. This one works great as an ending for a moderate tune with a shuffle rhythm. Similar to our scale exercise from Thursday, in which we worked with a 3rds sequence, this time we're harmonizing 3rds along strings 3 and 2. Each of the **dyads** (another word for double stop or two-note chord) on these strings is a 3rd interval. Notice that we're also introducing a **slide** on beat 3 of measure 1, indicated by the slanted lines. This tells you to start a fret or two below the target notes, pluck the strings, and quickly slide up to the target pitches at frets 4 and 3. Remember to maintain finger pressure on the fretboard throughout the slide so that the notes speak out. I play this riff fingerstyle, using my index and middle for the dyads on strings 3 and 2, my thumb for the open D string, and my ring finger for last note on string 1.

MON

Chord Vocabulary: We'll step outside the key of G this week by adding a few chords that work well in a common pattern. We have two voicings for G7, a G **augmented** chord (G+, which is like a G chord with a sharped 5th), a G6 (which could also be Em), and a Dm chord. The final chord, D7sus4, is similar to the Dsus4 from last week, but we have the note C on string 2 instead of the note D, which makes it a 7sus4. You'll see how three of these are commonly used together in Wednesday's fingerstyle workout.

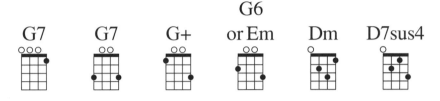

G7 G7 G+ G6 or Em Dm D7sus4

TUE

Strumming: This week, we're going to strum the same rhythm we did last week, but we'll use a shuffle feel and some different chords. Try strumming with your index finger on this one. When transitioning from G5 in measure 1 to Dm in measure 2, there's no need to lift up all your fret-hand fingers. If you fret G5 with your ring finger on string 2 and your pinky on string 3, you can leave your ring finger at that same fret for the Dm chord. This is called a **common tone** (the same note used in two different chords), and it makes for smoother chord transitions when we can exploit them by using the same fret-hand finger for both chords. You see the same thing in the last measure; you can use the same finger (pinky or ring) for the G note on string 1 in both G and C chords. This example also makes use of **first and second endings**. Play through measure 4 to the repeat sign and go back to the beginning. Then, when you get to measure 4 the second time, you skip over that measure (with the "1." bracket) to the measure with the "2." bracket.

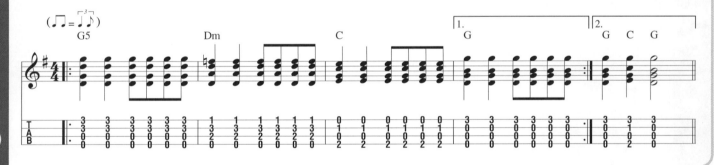

WED

Fingerstyle: Here we're using another rolling eighth-note fingerstyle pattern that starts low with the thumb and then cascades down through the fingers. The chord progression begins with a common pattern, G–G+–G6–G7, which creates an ascending chromatic line on string 4: D–D#–E–F. In measure 6, we see a *rit.* marking, which stands for **ritard**. This tells you to gradually slow down. Make sure to keep your fingers arched and use your fingertips for the notes on string 4 so the open G string is allowed to ring clearly.

THU

Scale Exercise: This is another G major scale sequence that's descending in groups of four notes at a time. When we start to get into longer streams of notes like this, several plucking options arise. You can alternate your index and middle fingers, you can alternate a finger (index or middle) with your thumb, or you can alternate downstrokes and upstrokes with your thumb, as if it were a plectrum. This is a bit easier to do if have a bit of a nail on your thumb, but it's possible without it as well. You just have to get a feel for it. If you work on this method, the motion should come from your first joint—not the second. In other words, the thumb shouldn't bend in half; it should move as one solid unit. For this exercise at this tempo, I tend to alternate my i and m fingers, but you should experiment to see what feels best for you.

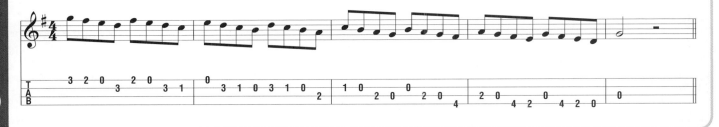

FRI

Legato: This exercise is similar to last week, but we're working on mixing legato with plucked notes and faster notes with slower ones. We're using the same combination of plucking and pull-offs for each string set: pluck, pull-off, pluck, pluck. Considering this, I use the same plucking-hand fingers throughout: i and m. This pattern is included in the music, but feel free to try another method if it feels more natural. Concentrate on keeping a steady tempo throughout, making sure that the pulled-off notes aren't rushed and that the sustained half notes receive their full duration.

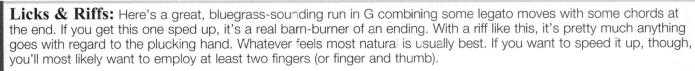

SAT

Licks & Riffs: Here's a great, bluegrass-sounding run in G combining some legato moves with some chords at the end. If you get this one sped up, it's a real barn-burner of an ending. With a riff like this, it's pretty much anything goes with regard to the plucking hand. Whatever feels most natural is usually best. If you want to speed it up, though, you'll most likely want to employ at least two fingers (or finger and thumb).

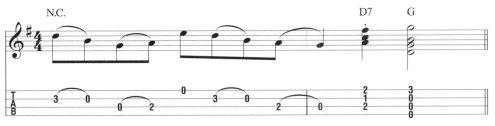

SUN

Miscellaneous: This week we're introducing two new musical concepts. The first appears at the very beginning: the **octave**. Notice that we're playing a G note on the open G string and one on fret 3 of string 1; these two notes are one octave apart. We're using an open string here, but this shape can be made moveable very easily, as demonstrated with the chord frames. It's the same shape whether you're using strings 3 and 1 or strings 4 and 2. The note on the higher string is just three frets higher than the one on the lower string. The remainder of the riff is a blues turnaround that kind of works backwards through the chromatic line on string 4 we saw in the example on Wednesday. The second musical concept is the **triplet**. These are eighth-note triplets, which means we're playing three eighth notes in a beat instead of two. Listen to the audio to hear how these sound. Notice that we end with a G7 chord, which is characteristic of the blues.

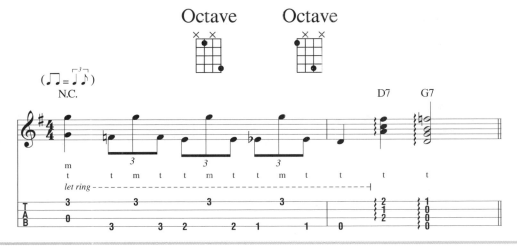

MON

Chord Vocabulary: This week we'll learn a few more chords outside of the key of G and a few variations on those within it. E7 is an easy one-finger chord, and Em7 (which could also be G6) is as easy as they come! We have two variations on a C chord: Csus2 and Csus4. But, wasn't this Csus2 chord called Gsus4 in Week 3? Good eye! Yes it was. It turns out that any sus4 chord can also be called a sus2 chord from another root, and vice versa. Suspended chords are funny like that. The musical context will usually tell you which name makes more sense. Finally, we have Dm7 and F, both of which contain our first partial **barre**. This is represented by the curved line in the grid, which tells us to play both strings by "barring" one finger (our index, in this case) across them. The F chord is also our first totally **moveable voicing**, because it contains no open strings.

E7   Em7 or G6   Csus2   Csus4   Dm7   F

TUE

Strumming: We'll use the E7 and F chords in a new strumming pattern that makes use of **syncopation**, or the stressing of a weak beat. Pay attention to the strumming direction marks in the music and follow them closely. This will result in pairing downstrokes with downbeats, which is the best way to maintain a strong rhythmic feel without having to think about it. Keep your strumming hand moving in a steady down and up motion throughout, but you'll purposefully be missing the strings on some of the strokes to create the syncopation. This purposeful missing of the strings is called a "ghost stroke" and is represented by the downstroke symbol in parentheses.

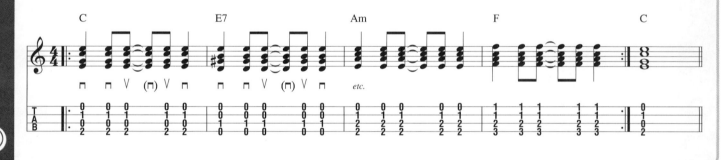

WED

Fingerstyle: In keeping with the syncopation theme from yesterday, this fingerpicking pattern is syncopated as well, accenting the "and" of beat 2. This is created by playing a t-i-m pattern (a three-note group) two times in a row. We round it out with r and m at the end to complete the pattern. You can hear how, in this instance, it makes sense to call the first chord a Csus2 instead of Gsus4, since the whole riff revolves around the C chord.

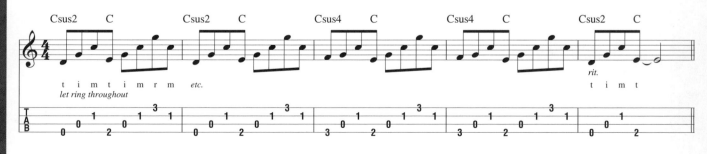

THU

Scale Exercise: This week we're changing keys to work with a C major scale instead of G major. We'll start with the highest note we can play in open position (G on fret 3, string 1) and play all the way down to the lowest note (the open D string). Then we'll come back up to the tonic C note on string 2.

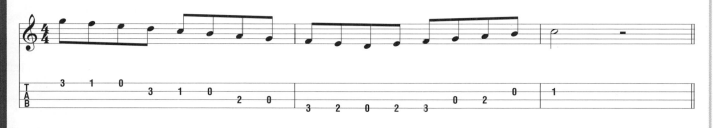

FRI

Legato: Let's try our legato skills within the context of a chord now. This is a great way to add some interest to your playing. Instead of just strumming a chord, you can strum a chord with one of the notes unfretted and then hammer it on. Or you can use the same idea with pull-offs. Start with the Csus2 voicing from Monday. Strum through the strings and then hammer onto fret 2 of string 4 with your middle finger, allowing all the other strings to continue ringing. In measure 2, begin with the same chord (though it's now called Gsus4 because of what follows), strum through the strings, and then pull off your index finger to sound the open B string on beat 2.

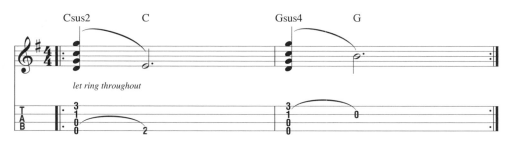

SAT

Licks & Riffs: Here's a great lick in C that also has a bit of a bluegrass sound to it. It begins with a **pickup note**, which is simply a note that precedes the downbeat—in this case, by an eighth note. On the downbeat, we have a chromatic **passing tone**, G♭, in between the G and F notes, which lends a bit of a jazzy flavor. Remember that you need to have your index finger planted on the first fret before you pull off from the second fret.

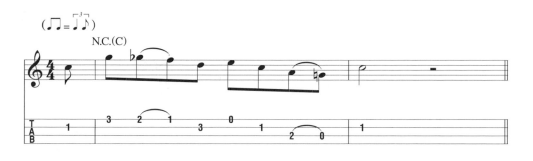

SUN

Miscellaneous: We'll work in the key of C for this one and introduce another concept: the **quarter-step bend**. When we bend strings on the ukulele (or on a guitar or bass), the pitch goes up. The more you bend the string, the more the pitch rises. By giving just a slight tug on it, we raise it enough to be "in the cracks," or between two pitches on adjacent frets. In this example, we're fretting a double stop of an E♭ note on fret 4, string 2 with our middle finger and G on fret 3, string 1 with our index finger. While holding those notes down, push string 2 a bit up toward the ceiling with your middle finger. You should hear the pitch rise a bit. You'll do this again at the end with the B♭ note on string 3, fret 3. For this note, however, you can either push it up (toward the ceiling) or pull it down (toward the floor) to bend it; either method will produce the same result. For bluesy riffs like this, I tend to pluck everything with my thumb because I like the sound of it.

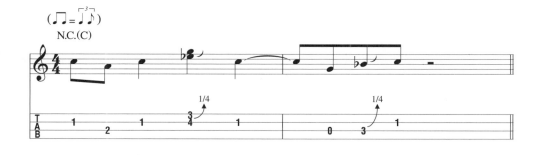

MON

Chord Vocabulary: This week we have two versions for C7: a moveable voicing (no open strings) and a partial open voicing. Gm is presented as an open chord with a barre, and we also see G in its moveable form in third position. Compare this to the F chord from last week, and you'll see that the G chord is just two frets higher than the F. In fact, both of these chords are actually E-form barre chords. Why? Take a look at the E chord back in Week 1. Does the shape look familiar? Try playing it with your ring finger on string 4, your middle finger on string 3, and your index finger barring the open strings behind the nut. Do you see it now? These moveable F and G chords are the same exact shape as the open E chord; it's just that in the open E chord, we're using the open strings, so you don't have to barre them. Finally, we have an open version of Bm and a moveable version: an A-form Bm chord. Compare this moveable Bm to the open Am chord from Week 2, and you should see the same logic at work.

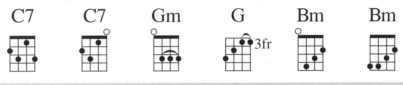

TUE

Strumming: This pattern is similar to last week's syncopated pattern, but we've added an extra eighth note in beat 1. We're also alternating every other measure with another pattern that's not syncopated. Therefore, we could say we have a two-measure strum pattern. Don't miss the staccato markings in measures 2, 4, 6, and 7, as they're part of this riff's appeal. After you strum the chord, quickly touch the strings with your strumming-hand palm to silence them and create the staccato sound.

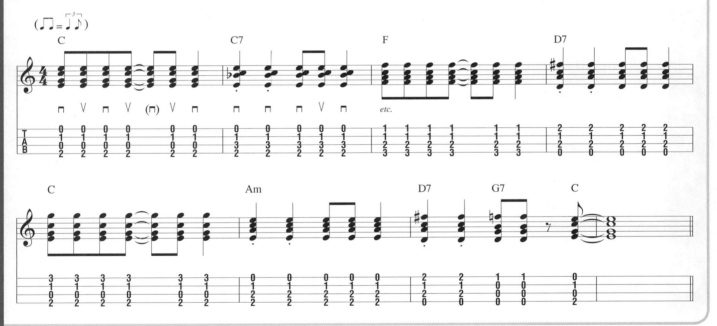

WED

Fingerstyle: This week we're using a rolling fingerpicking pattern in triplets—just straight up and down through the strings. As such, a t–i–m–r–m–i fingering approach works best. Another lesson here deals with the partial fretting of chords. When moving from the G chord to the Bm chord, for example, instead of trying to put all four fingers of the Bm down at once, you can add them one or two at a time. If you use your middle or index finger for the high G note on fret 3, string 1, you can start the Bm chord on beat 3 with only your ring and pinky fingers in place (on fret 4, string 4 and fret 4, string 3, respectively). Then you can get your middle and index fingers in place while plucking the F♯ and B notes on strings 4 and 3. When strumming chords, of course, you need to (usually) have all the notes in place, and many times we'll cheat a bit by beginning to change chords on the eighth note before the new chord. But when fingerpicking, every note is important, and we generally want the pattern to sound as flowing as possible. The concept of partial fretting can really aid in this pursuit.

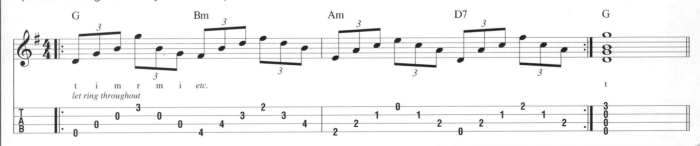

THU

Scale Exercise: We're working with the C major scale again in open position this week, but we're throwing a monkey wrench into the rhythm by mixing in a quarter note on beat 1. Be sure you're not rushing the quarter notes; tap your foot along with the beat as you play. I tend to alternate my index and middle fingers for the plucking here, but you can try the alternating thumb method as well.

FRI

Legato: We'll look at more chordal legato work here, using our new G minor chord. For the Gm chord, barre fret 3 with your index finger on strings 1–3. Strum the chord and hammer on to fret 5, string 3 with your ring finger. Be precise with your hammer-on so that strings 1, 2, and 4 are allowed to ring out. For the D chord, I like to slide my index-finger barre down to the second fret, play fret 3, string 2 with my ring finger, and hammer on to fret 3 with my middle finger. In measure 2, you have a hammer-on and pull-off strung together on string 3. I use my thumb for plucking throughout. For the last two notes—the F♯ on fret 4, string 4 and the open G string—use a smooth continuous motion with the thumb. In other words, after plucking the F♯ note on string 4, allow the thumb to continue its motion down to the G string so it can pluck it.

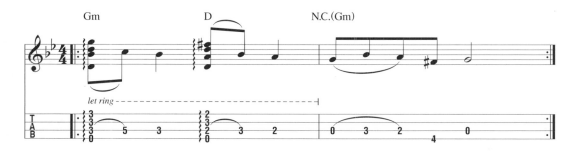

SAT

Licks & Riffs: We're seeing our first 16th notes in this riff, which uses pull-offs in a G minor phrase. You can count 16th notes as: "1 e and a, 2 e and a," etc. One thing to watch with this riff is the pull-off from B♭ to the open G string. If you're not careful, you can accidentally nudge the open B string while you're pulling off, which will not sound good at all here. To prevent this, I usually keep my index finger lightly touching string 2 after playing the C note at fret 1. That way, even if I do nudge string 2 while pulling off on string 3, it remains silent.

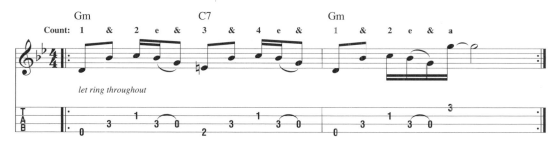

SUN

Miscellaneous: We're working with another bend this week, but this time it's a half-step bend. This means we'll be pushing the string up a bit more to match the note that's one fret higher. In this case, we're bending the note D at fret 3, string 2 up a half step to E♭. To make sure your intonation is right, you should play the E♭ note at fret 4, string 2 first and then bend fret 3 to match that pitch. Since this lick has a country-blues flavor to it, we're being a little lazy with the bend and not getting up to the E♭ right away, but we are getting there. Notice that the lick in measure 2 is almost exactly the same as the one in Saturday's workout from Week 5. Again, I use my thumb to pluck every note here.

WEEK 7

BARITONE UKULELE AEROBICS

MON

Chord Vocabulary: This week we're adding a moveable minor chord shape, Fm, which is an E-form barre chord. (Compare this shape to the Em chord in Week 2 to see what I mean.) We then have two more variations on the open Em chord: Em7 and Em6. You may see this Em6 chord called an A7 at times; again, this depends on musical context. Finally, we have two moveable versions of Am7 and Am6.

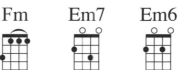

TUE

Strumming: These m7 and m6 chords are great to use when you want to create some motion instead of just hanging on one chord for four measures. For example, here we see a common way to use Am7 and Am6 along with Am. The strum pattern is another combination of quarter and eighth notes. Don't worry too much about hitting only strings 4 and 3 on beat 1 of each measure. You really just want to avoid string 1 for sure because we're going for a low–high sound on beats 1 and 2. You could hit only string 4 or strings 4–2 on beat 1 and it will still sound alright. Just try to not strum through the whole chord on that beat.

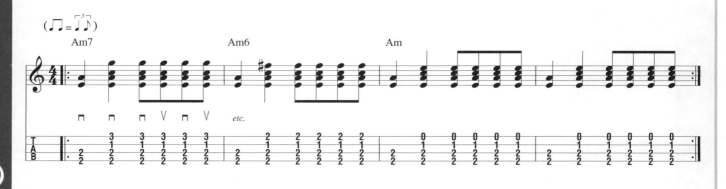

WED

Fingerstyle: This week we'll get into the block-chord fingerstyle technique. This means that, instead of picking through the chord one string at a time in arpeggio fashion, we'll use our thumb, index, middle, and ring fingers together to pluck all four strings at the same time. Plant your thumb on string 4, index on string 3, middle on string 2, and ring on string 1 and use this plucking arrangement throughout. You might not think so, but this will result in a very different sound than simply strumming the strings. To hear what I mean, try this example both ways: fingerstyle and strumming.

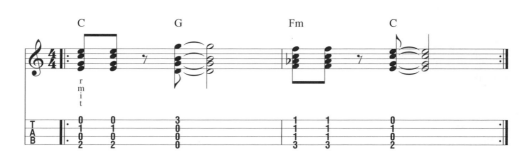

Scale Exercise: We're working out of the C major scale again this week, but we're upping the ante with a three-note sequence using triplets. Practice it slowly at first and make sure the tempo is steady throughout. I'm alternating my i and m fingers on this one, but you can try other picking methods if you'd like.

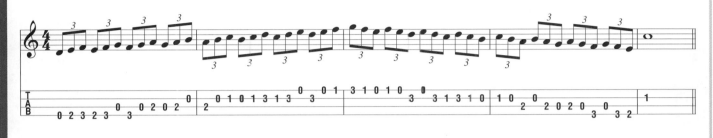

Legato: Here's a triplet exercise that focuses on repetitive hammer-ons and pull-offs to and from open strings. Strive for a clean tone with no extraneous notes—open strings or fretted ones—popping out during the hammers or pulls. Regarding the plucking hand, I use my thumb, index, and middle throughout, shifting over to the 3-2-1 string set in measure 3, but feel free to try other methods as well.

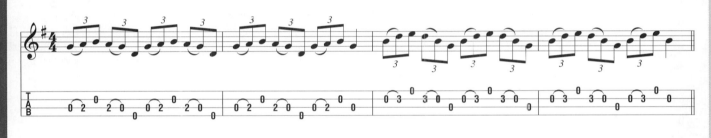

Licks & Riffs: We're combining our D chord form here with a fingerpicking pattern and legato moves on the top string to create a nice chordal arpeggio riff. The thumb will rock back and forth between strings 4 and 3, so watch the fingering between the staves. With the hammer-ons and pull-offs on the top string, be aware of two things: consistency of volume and steadiness of tempo.

Miscellaneous: This week we have a bluesy riff in a question-and-answer phrase with two different bends: a quarter-step bend on string 4 and a half-step bend on string 3. Again, check the pitch on the half-step bend against a fretted C note (either fret 1, string 2 or fret 5, string 3) to make sure you're getting it in tune. And don't over-bend the fourth string; the note should be "in between the cracks"—higher than fret 3 but lower than fret 4.

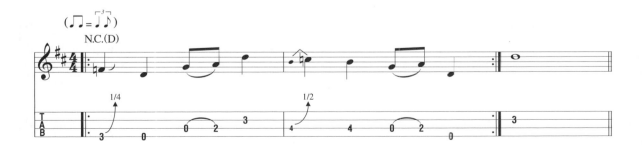

MON

Chord Vocabulary: Let's add a few more fancy-sounding chords to our arsenal this week. First we have open versions of Gadd9 and Eadd9. Then we have the moveable version of the Eadd9 with Fadd9; we simply moved the E chord form up one fret. To top it off, we have open versions of two major 7th chords: Fmaj7 and Dmaj7.

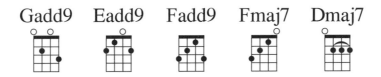

Gadd9   Eadd9   Fadd9   Fmaj7   Dmaj7

TUE

Strumming: Here's another shuffle pattern mixing quarter and eighth notes. Although there's no syncopation here, we've added an **accent** to beats 2 and 4 to create a **backbeat** feel. This simply means that you strum a bit harder on those beats, which helps the strum pattern come to life. You may want to experiment with fingerings for the Dmaj7 chord. You can either barre it (as shown in the chord grid on Monday) or use three different fingers. You may find that, when coming from the Gadd9 chord, the multiple finger approach works better for you. Again, don't worry about hitting only the bottom two strings on beat 1; just try to hit the lower strings.

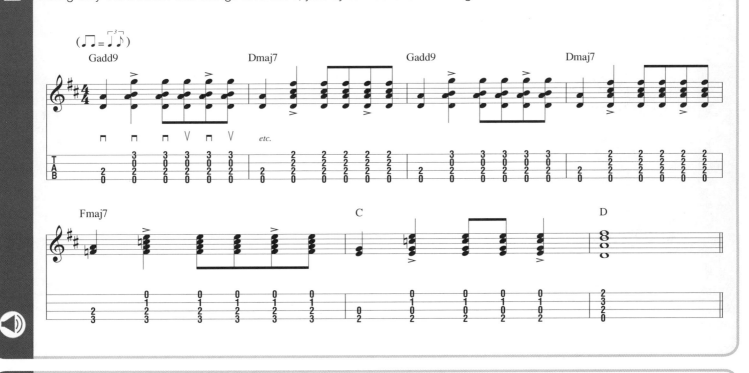

WED

Fingerstyle: This example is similar in technique to last week, but we've separated the lowest note (played by the thumb) from the fingers in a few of the chords. The progression is an interesting one in G major that contains two non-diatonic chords: Fadd9 and Eadd9. For the final G chord, strum through the strings with your thumb.

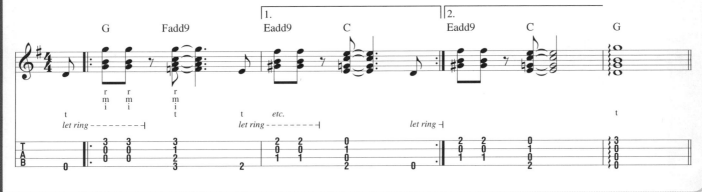

Scale Exercise: We're using the C major pentatonic scale here, which is the same as C major without the 4th and 7th degrees. It's spelled C–D–E–G–A. We've increased the tempo a bit, and we're also including a position shift. After playing measure 1 in first position, shift up to third position, playing fret 5, string 1 with your third finger and fret 3, string 1 with your first finger. While playing the open E string, shift back down to first position to finish the measure. Open strings can be quite handy for shifting positions like this.

Legato: We're increasing the difficulty level from last week's exercise here by using 16th notes (instead of triplets) with two hammer-ons or pull-offs in tandem. You should perform this entirely in first position—i.e., use your second and third fingers on string 3 and your first and third fingers on string 2. If you don't have the multiple hammer or pull technique down yet, it will definitely show on this one!

Licks & Riffs: Similarly to last week, we're adding hammer-ons to a fingerpicking pattern to dress it up a bit. This time we're using triplets in a shuffle feel. Notice also the use of common tones—C on string 2 and the open E on string 1—in this progression. This results in a very connected, flowing sound. However, in order to take advantage of this, you must keep the C note on string 2 fretted the whole time. Don't pick it up when moving from chord to chord!

Miscellaneous: This week we return to the idea of moving one note in a chord to create different harmonies. This is an idea we first looked at on Sunday's workouts in Weeks 1 and 2, but now we'll put some of our more sophisticated harmonies at work to create a common minor progression and play it fingerstyle. In order to maintain the best continuity between the chords, remember to take advantage of common tones. The open E string is a common tone, but so is the E note on string 4. So be sure to use the same finger for that note throughout the progression. For me, that means starting with the middle finger on string 4 and the pinky on string 2. From there, everything falls into place without having to move the middle finger.

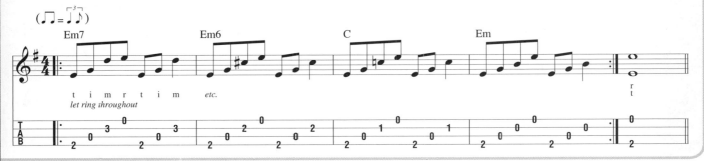

MON

Chord Vocabulary: Let's look at a few more 6th chords this week. First we have an open E6 and then a moveable version with F6. Next is A6, which is a moveable version of the open G6 (or Em7) we saw in Week 5. Again, any major 6th chord could also be named a minor chord with a different root (or a minor 7th, depending on the notes it contains). The next chord, F#m6, is a moveable version of the Em6 from Week 7, and finally we have an open Dm6 and its moveable barred version as Em6.

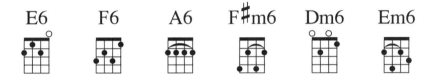

E6   F6   A6   F#m6   Dm6   Em6

TUE

Strumming: Here's a quicker shuffled strum pattern that makes extensive use of staccato and adds some syncopation as well. Keep the strums nice and clipped sounding for maximum effect. I tend to strum this one with my thumb, for two reasons: 1) I just prefer the sound of it for this type of thing, and 2) it's a bit easier to mute the strings with my palm immediately after strumming with my thumb as opposed to the index finger. Note also the alternate chord names in parentheses: A6 = F#m7, and Am6 = F#m7♭5. Although we haven't seen a m7♭5 chord in our Monday workouts yet, as seen here, a m6 chord can also be named a m7♭5 from a different root.

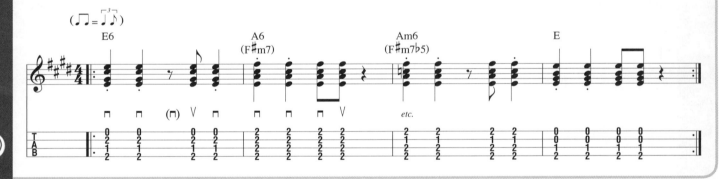

WED

Fingerstyle: We're expanding on last week's fingerstyle workout here by adding a percussive element. On beats 2 and 4 (the backbeat), plant your plucking-hand fingers on the strings—thumb on string 4, index on string 3, etc.—with a good amount of force to create a "tick" sound. This simulates a snare drum that's played with a brush and really helps to enforce the groove. When you get this going well, it has a great "one-man-band" feel to it. Be sure to note that—aside from the added percussive ticks—this example uses the same pluck-hand technique as last week.

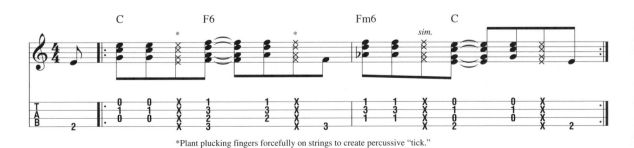

*Plant plucking fingers forcefully on strings to create percussive "tick."

THU

Scale Exercise: We're working from the C major pentatonic or A minor pentatonic scale (they contain the same notes) again this week, focusing on moving vertically through the strings smoothly. The fret hand can remain in first position through the whole example; the challenge will likely be with the plucking hand. Again, I alternate the i and m fingers for this one, but try alternating with the thumb if it feels better.

FRI

Legato: It's a pull-off extravaganza this week. We're using the D major scale and are firmly planted in second position here. Use your index finger for fret 2, middle for fret 3, and pinky for fret 5 throughout. The only exception to this would possibly be on beat 3 in measure 2. Since we've just played fret 3 on string 2 with our middle finger, I prefer to use my ring finger for fret 3 on string 1 and pull off to my index finger, rather than flattening out my middle finger to play string 1. That's a personal preference, though; you should do what feels most natural (and sounds best) to you. Regarding the plucking hand, I use m and i on strings 1 and 2, respectively, throughout.

SAT

Licks & Riffs: Here's a great ending lick in F that has kind of a Western swing feel to it. After strumming the staccato F6 chord, you'll perform a **grace-note slide** from fret 3 to fret 4 on string 1. This means that the slide takes up no metric time; you just immediately slide from fret 3 to 4. I perform this slide with my third finger. The remainder of the lick can be handled nicely in first position, using a half barre at fret 1 for the beginning of measure 2. It ends with a bluesy device: a hammer-on from the minor 3rd (Ab) to the major 3rd (A) followed by the tonic F note. Regarding the plucking hand, there are a lot of possibilities here. I like to strum the first chord with my thumb and then use the thumb and index (or sometimes middle) finger for the remainder of the notes. But you can also handle this with just the index and middle fingers as well.

SUN

Miscellaneous: Let's work out with the grace-note slide a bit more today. In this example, we have ascending slides on strings 3 and 2 and then a descending slide on string 2. Descending slides are less common, but they sound great in bluesier styles. The tempo here is slow enough that you don't need to be terribly worried about fingering (on either hand, for that matter), but I like to fret measure 2 entirely with the second finger, sliding up from fret 2 to fret 3 and then moving back to fret 2 for the pull-off to the open G string. But feel free to change that up if it doesn't feel right to you. On the plucking hand, I use the thumb on string 4 and fingers for the rest of the notes.

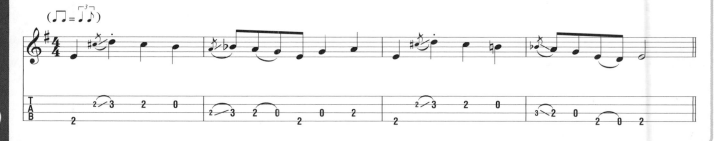

MON

Chord Vocabulary: Let's get a few more moveable shapes under our fingers this week. First we have an open D6 chord, which is a great-sounding alternative to D, especially as a V chord in the key of G. The barred moveable version of this chord is shown as E6 next. Note that these chords could also go by the names of Bm7 and C#m7, respectively, if the note on string 2 were treated as the root. Following is an A-form Bb chord in first position. Then we have a G-form A barre chord in second position. Finally, the D barre chord in second position is a C-form chord.

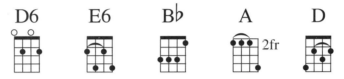

TUE

Strumming: This strumming pattern in G mixes shuffled eighth notes with a half rest each measure. It's a catchy little rhythm, but it also makes a good tempo exercise to make sure you're not rushing through the rests. We have our new D6 chord here as well as another new one: Cm. Although we haven't officially added this to our chord vocabulary, we did learn this moveable form back in Week 6 as a Bm in second position. This Cm is the same chord only one fret higher.

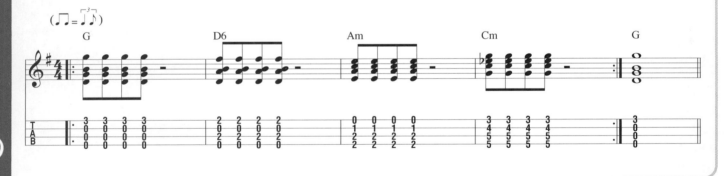

WED

Fingerstyle: Here's another take on the block-chord technique in which we're separating the thumb and fingers of the plucking hand in yet another way. Tap your foot along with the beat so you allow the tied notes their full rhythmic duration. We're using our new E6 and D6 chords here and, although you have plenty of time to make the chord change, you may want to try using your ring and pinky fingers for the D6 chord, as this will simply allow you to slide them down from the E6 chord. However, it's not critical in this example.

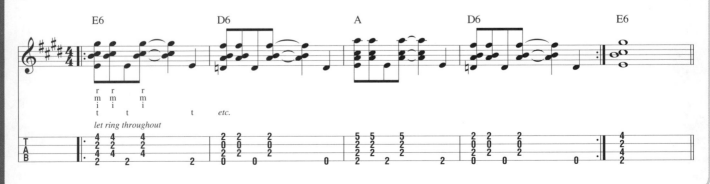

THU

Scale Exercise: Here we introduce a new scale: F major. We're simply running up (to a high G) and down in constant eighth notes, but each major scale in open position presents its own unique arrangement of scale tones per string, so they're all good practice.

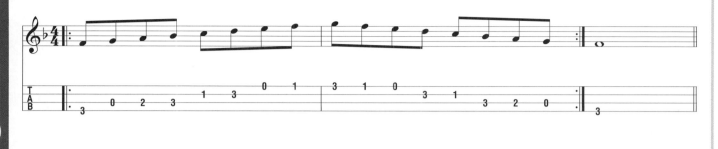

FRI

Legato: This is basically the opposite of last week's example. We're using all the same notes, but we're hammering from the open E string instead of pulling off to it. Again, concentrate on keeping a steady tempo throughout.

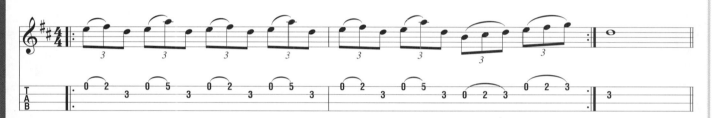

SAT

Licks & Riffs: Let's put our new Bb chord to use with a mysterious-sounding fingerstyle riff. By pulling off to the open E string, we create a tart Bbadd#11 harmony. We follow this by hammering onto fret 1 from the open E. Make sure the volume of all the notes on string 1 is consistent throughout, and keep the middle, ring, and pinky fret-hand fingers planted on strings 4, 3, and 2, respectively, throughout.

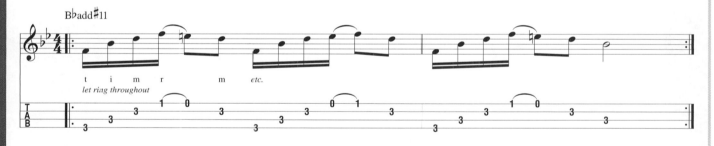

SUN

Miscellaneous: Building on the grace-note slides from last week, we're using double stops this week with a similar riff in E. I tend to use my middle and ring fret-hand fingers for all of the notes in measure 1, holding them together to work as one unit throughout the slides. But you can experiment with other fingerings if that doesn't feel good to you. The first slide is just like last week except in double-stop form. But for the slide on beat 4 of measure 1, you'll first perform a grace-note slide from fret 2 to 3 and then, without releasing fret-hand pressure or re-plucking the string, you'll slide down to fret 2 and sustain the notes across the bar line. This may take a bit of practice to get down, but remember that you have to maintain pressure with your fret hand in order to sustain the sliding notes. Regarding the plucking hand, I use my m and r fingers for all the double stops, but other possibilities would work fine as well.

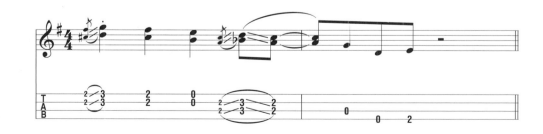

MON

Chord Vocabulary: This week we'll learn some more dominant 7th chord voicings, which always come in handy for numerous styles. First is A7, which is the moveable form of the open G7 from Week 4. E7 is the moveable form of open D7 from Week 2. The B7 chord is actually the open form of the moveable C7 that we encountered in Week 6, and F7 is the moveable form of the open E7 from Week 5.

A7   E7   B7   F7

TUE

Strumming: Here's a Dixieland-style workout using the chords we just learned. Notice that we use two different moveable forms of the open E7 chord: F#7 (first ending) and F7 (second ending). Be sure to note the staccato markings, as they're integral to the bouncy rhythm. I like to strum this one with my thumb, but the index finger works well too.

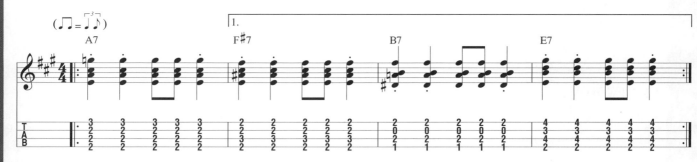

WED

Fingerstyle: Here's another fairly common block-chord approach: alternating chords on the downbeats with bass notes on the upbeats. Your picking-hand r, m, and i fingers should be locked together and acting as one cohesive unit. This technique produces a piano-like sound when done well. Again, experiment with different fret-hand fingerings to see which produces the smoothest transitions from chord to chord.

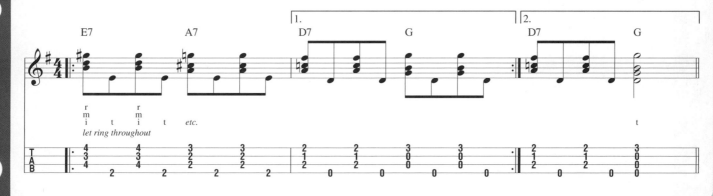

THU

Scale Exercise: We'll stick with the same F major scale as last week and work through it with a sequence in which a triplet figure is built off each note of the scale. This is a great exercise with which to alternate the starting plucking finger when using an i-m technique. In other words, alternate i and m fingers throughout the whole exercise, first starting on the i finger. Then play it again, this time starting on the m finger. Is one way easier than the other? Which areas tend to trip you up? Be sure to start slowly and work it up to speed only when you've truly got it under your fingers.

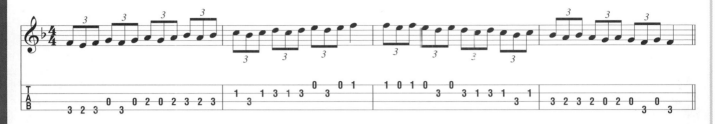

FRI

Legato: Here's a good, solid workout with the F major scale that's deceptively difficult to make sound smooth and steady. You'll remain firmly in first position until the very last ascending set of hammer-ons at the end of measure 4. At that point, you'll need to stretch out your fret-hand fingers, hammering from your index on fret 1 to your middle at fret 3 and your pinky at fret 5. Alternatively, some people prefer to use their ring finger for fret 3 on a move like this. Try both options to see what feels better.

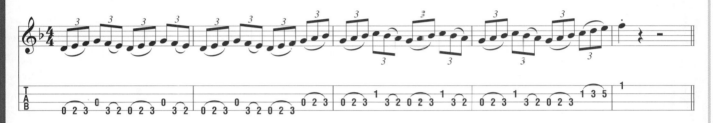

SAT

Licks & Riffs: Expanding on last week's arpeggio/legato combination, this is a nice, rolling arpeggio riff that uses a hammer-on/pull-off combination on string 1 for each chord. The E7 chord isn't too difficult; you just have to be precise with the pinky to make sure the G# on fret 4, string 1 is clear. But the A7 chord is trickier. You have a few different fret-hand options. If you're able to do it, you can barre fret 2 on strings 4–2 with your index finger and then bend it at the knuckle to allow string 1 to ring out, performing the hammer/pull move with either the middle or ring finger. If that's not doable for you, then you have two more options for fretting the notes on strings 4–2: index (string 4), middle (string 3), and ring (string 2), or middle (string 4), index (string 3), and ring (string 2). Either way, you'll need to hammer and pull with the pinky. I prefer the latter method (middle-index-ring), but try them all out to see what feels best.

SUN

Miscellaneous: Slides aren't just limited to single notes or double stops. We can slide entire chords around, as you'll see here. Remember to maintain full fret-hand pressure so all the notes speak out during the slide. I strum this one with either my thumb or index—whichever strikes my fancy at the time. It sounds great with either.

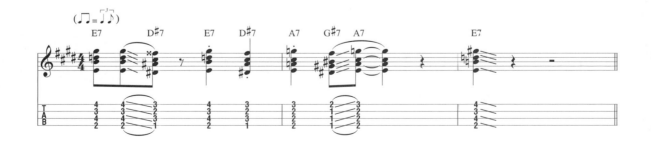

WEEK 12

MON

Chord Vocabulary: Let's learn a somewhat new chord type this week: the m7♭5 chord. I say "somewhat new" because this is another chord that goes by a different name depending on which note is considered the root. These could also be minor 6th chords of a different root in this regard. Therefore, the Dm6 and Em6 chords you learned in Week 9, for example, could also be called Bm7♭5 and C#m7♭5, respectively. We had to backtrack a little bit with regards to the G#m7 because we hadn't yet learned it as an open form. It's not nearly as common as Am7, so I presented it (the moveable version of the open G#m7) first. Then we see the open G#m7♭5 followed by its moveable form in Am7♭5. And if two names for one chord is not enough for you, don't fret. These chords can also be named as rootless ninth chords. We'll take a look at that idea a bit later.

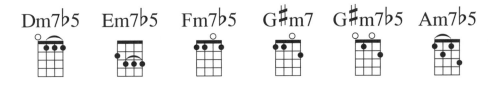

Dm7♭5   Em7♭5   Fm7♭5   G#m7   G#m7♭5   Am7♭5

TUE

Strumming: Let's put one of our new m7♭5 chords into practice with our first strumming pattern in **3/4 time**: three beats per measure. Follow the strumming direction marks using either your thumb or index finger.

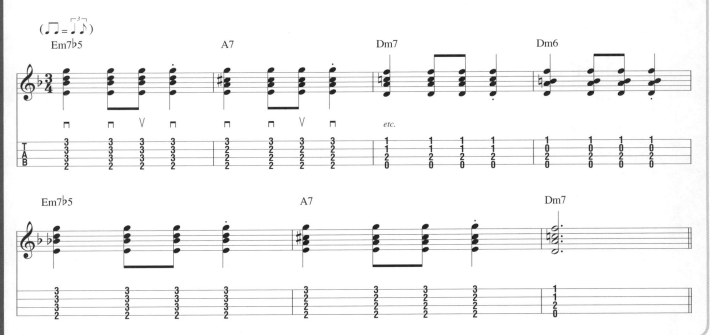

WED

Fingerstyle: This is the same pattern as last week, but we're using staccato throughout for an entirely different effect. After each pluck with the fingers or thumb, immediately plant them back on the strings to stop them from ringing. The E♭6 chord is another moveable version of D6 you learned in Week 10 (when you also learned the moveable version as E6). It could also be called a Cm7 chord if you treated the C note on string 2 as the root. Notice the smooth **voice leading** throughout this example. There's minimal movement between the notes in the first three chords. This results in a very smooth sound.

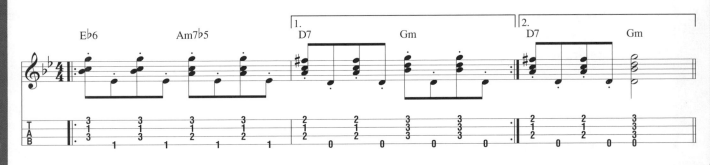

THU

Scale Exercise: We're just descending and ascending the F major scale again this week, but there's a twist: we're playing each note twice. This may not seem like a big deal because your fret hand is actually moving more slowly, but there's a unique coordination that goes with this type of thing, so it's important to make sure both hands are in sync. All of the notes should sound clear and full. It's not uncommon in this type of thing for the first or second instance of each note to sound clipped or shanked a bit, which happens when the hands drift out of sync.

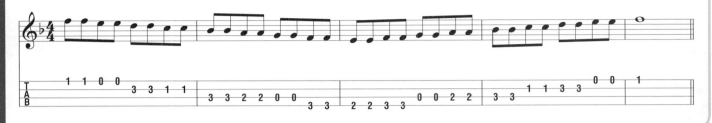

FRI

Legato: Today we'll push our legato technique into new territory by using hammer-ons and pull-offs on two strings at once. The hardest part of this technique is keeping the finger on the lower-pitched string clear of the higher one when pulling off. For instance, in measures 3–4 and 7–8, you don't want to nudge string 2 when pulling off on string 3 (or when hammering on, for that matter). This will take a bit of practice, but you'll get it.

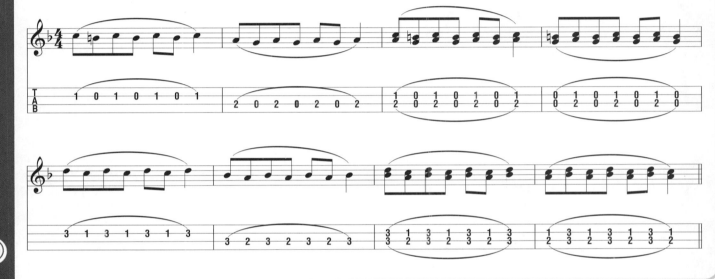

SAT

Licks & Riffs: Here's a nice little riff using our Em7♭5 chord, a barred A7 chord, and a bluesy pull-off riff in D minor. I play this riff fingerstyle, but you could strum the chords just as well if you'd like.

SUN

Miscellaneous: Here's another common chord-sliding move: separating the chord and bass note and sliding up into the chord from a half step below. When you repeat these three things—bass note, chord a half step below, and the target chord—in a straight eighth-note rhythm, you get a nice, bluesy, ragtime-style riff. For the fret hand, use your middle finger on string 3 and an index-finger half barre on strings 2 and 1. The G bass note on string 4 can be played by your ring or pinky finger—whichever feels more comfortable to you.

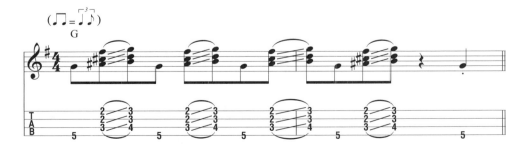

31

MON

Chord Vocabulary: Let's expand our knowledge of dominant chords with some more 7sus4 options. First the open G7sus4 is followed by a moveable version, A7sus4, in second position. For the open G7sus4, you may find it better to barre strings 1 and 2 or fret them individually, depending on the context. The E7sus4 form is shown in first position as F7sus4, which requires a full barre with the index finger. Finally, we have the open B7sus4 and its moveable version, C7sus4. I'd recommend fretting B7sus4 with the second, third, and fourth fingers so that the moveable form will be just as easy to play.

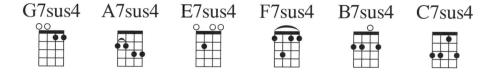

TUE

Strumming: All of the 7sus4 chords we learned on Monday can be nicely alternated with standard 7th chords, as we'll see here. This is a cycle of 5ths progression in F major, in which each chord is followed by one a 5th below it. Each dominant chord is first presented as a 7sus4 and then a normal 7th chord. You'll want to experiment with the fret-hand fingering of each to see what feels most natural to you.

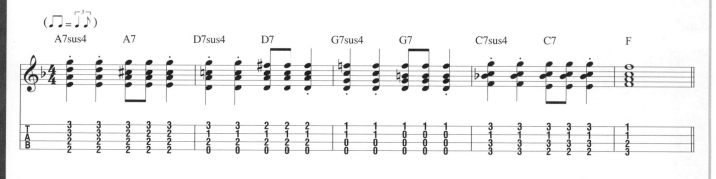

WED

Fingerstyle: This week we'll start tackling a few more challenging arpeggio patterns. Here's a nice-sounding one that uses a very specific plucking-hand pattern, so pay careful attention to the fingering shown. Notice that we're repeating a three-note pattern (t-i-m) in straight 16th notes, which results in a syncopation known as a **hemiola**: a three-against-four feel. This continues for three beats. In order to "right the ship," as it were, we temporarily break the pattern on beat 4 and add an extra note plucked with i so that the pattern can start again in measure 2 with the thumb. Notice also that, although the i and m fingers remain on strings 2 and 1 throughout, respectively, the thumb alternates between strings 4 and 3. Take this one slowly at first until you've got the fingerpicking pattern solid.

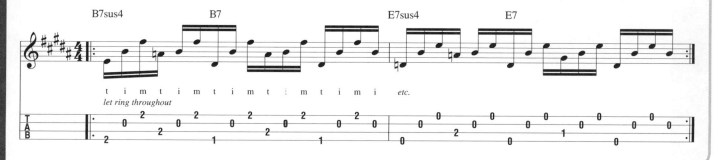

Scale Exercise: As a variation on last week's exercise, we're repeating a simple two-note sequence throughout the F major scale in open position here. Be sure to keep the hands in perfect sync throughout; this will likely mean you'll need to start fairly slowly to get the coordination down.

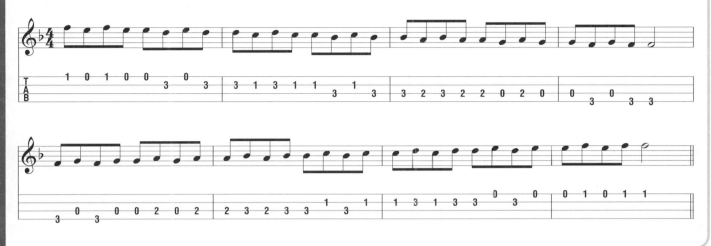

Legato: We're expanding the concept of slurring two notes at once here by working in A major and employing some different fret-hand combinations, including an index barre in measures 1 and 3. I've added fret-hand fingerings to the music for you to follow. In measure 3, you'll need to hammer and pull with your ring and pinky fingers, which may take a little practice. I'm plucking all of these dyads with my i and m fingers, but you can use another method if you'd like.

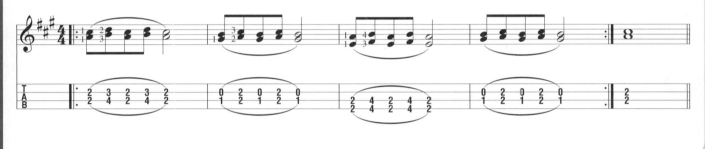

Licks & Riffs: Here's a cool-sounding riff in D minor that demonstrates the close link between a minor 7th chord and a 7sus4 chord that's a 4th above. In this case, we're talking about Dm7 and G7sus4. In fact, the only difference between Dm7 and G7sus4 is that Dm7 has an A note whereas G7sus4 has a G note. The other three notes—D, F, and C—are common in both chords. Be sure to let the notes ring in this one and don't miss the staccato markings on the G7sus4 chord in measure 2. I pluck all the notes on strings 4 and 3 with my thumb here and use my i and m fingers for strings 2 and 1, respectively.

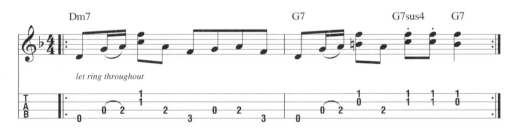

Miscellaneous: This week we'll take a look at a specific plucking-hand technique called **tremolo**. This simply means that you're picking a note repeatedly as fast as possible. There are different ways to achieve tremolo, but here we're going to use the thumb. Plant your plucking-hand fingers on the face of the uke to brace your hand and extend your thumb in a straight line so that the knuckle is not bent. Wiggle it from the bottom joint (the one attached to your hand) back and forth as fast as possible to achieve the effect. It'll take some practice for sure to get it, but it's a really nice sound and well worth the effort.

MON

Chord Vocabulary: This week we'll check out a new chord type: the minor add9 chord. This is a hauntingly beautiful chord that can really add serious character to a piece. The open Em(add9) is followed by the moveable Fm(add9), which is the most common moveable m(add9) form. The first Am(add9) is a rootless voicing, meaning there's no A note in the chord. The next one, in fifth position, takes advantage of the open strings to create a full lush-sounding Am(add9). The Dm(add9) chord is inverted, with its ♭3rd on the bottom. As such, you could also call this chord Fmaj13 (we'll see 13th chords later). Finally, we have the moveable version of this chord as an Em(add9) in second position. This one requires a little stretch, but it's not too bad.

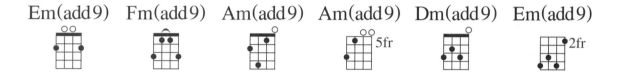

Em(add9)   Fm(add9)   Am(add9)   Am(add9) 5fr   Dm(add9)   Em(add9) 2fr

TUE

Strumming: Let's put our fifth-position Am(add9) chord to use with a shuffle strumming pattern. We're alternating between Am(add9) and Fmaj7 here, which share the open E string as a common tone. Even though the full chord is shown on the last eighth note of beats 1 and 2, we really cheat a bit and only strum the top one or two strings because we're taking the opportunity to shift down for the open Fmaj7 chord. You can do the same when shifting back to Am(add9) from Fmaj7. Strum with your thumb for this example, using a **rest stroke** for the bass note (beat 1) in each measure. In other words, pluck string 4 with your thumb and allow it to quickly come to rest against string 3. This will accomplish two things: 1) it will provide a clear single bass note on beat 1, which we want in this case, and 2) it will set you up for the strum that follows on beat 2 (strings 3–1).

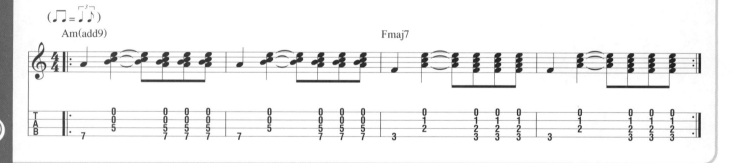

WED

Fingerstyle: Here's a Pink Floyd-sounding example using our open Em(add9) and Dm(add9) forms. Be sure to allow the open E string to ring out, as this is crucial to achieving the smooth, connected sound here.

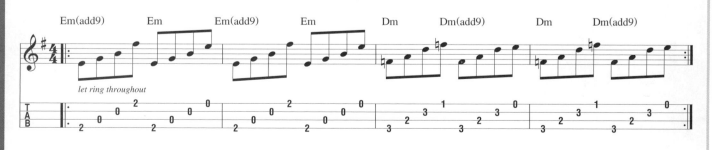

THU

Scale Exercise: To complement our new Em(add9) chord this week, we'll look at a scale that's tailor-made for it: the E minor **hexatonic** scale. This is a six-note scale—one more note than a pentatonic and one less than a major or minor scale. It lays out on the neck with an interesting pattern of three notes on the bottom and top strings and two notes on the middle two strings. Try alternating the i and m fingers of the plucking hand for this one. Start slowly at first and then work it up to speed.

FRI

Legato: This week we'll look at **oblique** legato techniques, in which one note remains stationary while another one moves. In our case, this means one note will be sustained while we perform hammer-ons and pull-offs on an adjacent string. Measures 1 and 2 shouldn't be terribly difficult; remember to keep your fingers arched to allow the open strings to ring. In measure 3, however, you'll need to barre strings 3 and 2 with your index finger at fret 2 and hammer and pull with your pinky on string 3 (since your ring finger will be fretting the F# note on string 4). Take it slowly and make sure you're getting a clear tone out of everything.

SAT

Licks & Riffs: Here's a nice-sounding descending lick using the E minor hexatonic scale with an included blue note (the grace-note slide from B♭ on string 3) for a sassy touch. We're mixing plucked and legato (pull-off) notes throughout, so be sure you're keeping a steady rhythm. Speaking of rhythm, it's a bit syncopated in the middle, so listen to the audio if you're having trouble getting it.

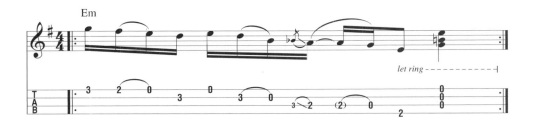

SUN

Miscellaneous: We're raising the difficulty level from last week a bit by tremolo picking two notes at once. This requires a bit broader motion with the thumb, but it's still the same basic technique. This kind of technique usually requires a bit of experimentation with how you hold your thumb, how your brace your hand with the other fingers, etc. It's a matter of trying different things out until you discover what works for you.

WEEK 15

MON

Chord Vocabulary: Let's look at more augmented chords this week. The open forms aren't difficult to play, but the moveable versions can be a little uncomfortable at first. The F+ requires your pinky to be on string 4, which is a bit of a rarity and will likely feel a little strange at first. Eb+ is a bit of a stretch but is playable unless your hands are really small. Just be sure to keep your fret-hand thumb behind the neck to increase your reach. A+ is the moveable version of the G+ we saw back in Week 4 and is quite a stretch as well.

E+   F+   D+   Eb+   A+

TUE

Strumming: Here's a strum pattern that mixes swung eighth notes with triplets throughout. Try both the suggested strum directions to see which feels best to you. Regarding the fret hand, there are a lot of possibilities, but I always try to use a common tone when changing chords if possible to achieve the smoothest transition. That said, I use my ring finger on string 4 (the E note) for all four chords: ring and index for E; ring, index, and middle (low to high) for E+; ring, middle, and pinky (low to high) for A; and ring, pinky, and middle (low to high) for Am.

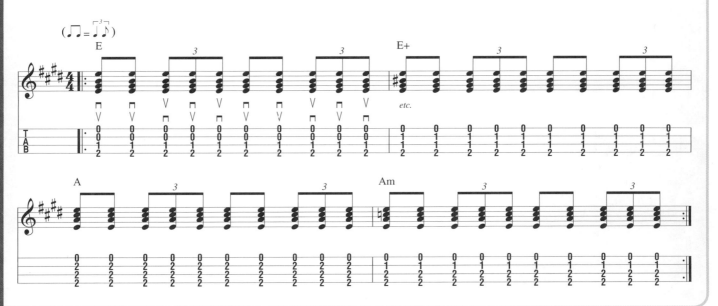

WED

Fingerstyle: This is a nice-sounding fingerpicking pattern in D that makes use of our open D+ chord. We're using a three-note descending pattern of m-i-t throughout, alternating our thumb on strings 3 and 4. An alternate fingering of index-pinky-middle (low to high) for the D chord will make it easier to transition to D+.

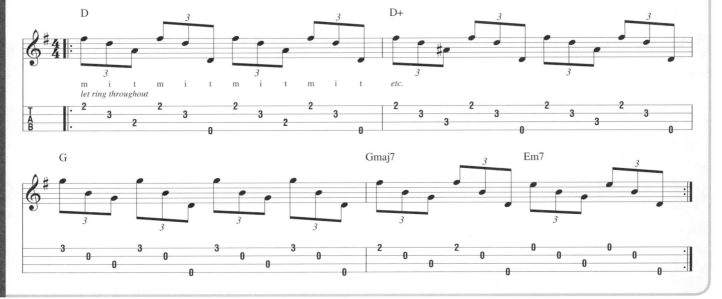

THU

Scale Exercise: We continue with the E minor hexatonic this week. This is a staggered, every-other-note sequence that would be called a 3rd sequence if it were a standard major or minor scale. Since there are only six notes, however, not all of the intervals are 3rds—some are 4ths—so we'll just call it staggered. Why the pull-off at the end of the first measure? Well, if you try playing this phrase with alternating i and m fingers, you'll see what I mean. If you begin with the m finger, the whole first measure lines up nicely. But if you didn't add that pull-off and continued alternating, you'd start measure 2 with the m finger as well (obviously). And look what happens next. You have m on string 4, i on string 3, m on string 4, and i on string 3. This is very awkward for the right hand and doesn't feel natural at all. Therefore, by adding the pull-off at the end of measure 1, we can start measure 2 with the i finger and alternate from there, after which the whole measure lines up nicely for the plucking hand. Consequently, if I were going to loop this phrase—in other words, repeat measures 1 and 2—I would pull off from the first G note to the open E string, as this would allow me to get back on track by leading with the m finger again.

FRI

Legato: We continue with the oblique motion this week, using different chord forms and legato combinations. I fret measures 1–3 with my middle finger on string 4 throughout, which means I use my ring and pinky fingers for the legato moves over the A chords. In measure 4, I fret the B7 chord with my index on string 4 and ring finger on string 3, as this allows me to hammer and pull fret 2 with my middle finger. Be sure the legato notes are all speaking out clearly before you speed this one up.

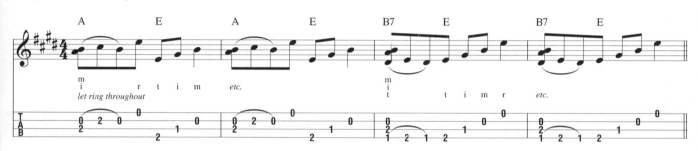

SAT

Licks & Riffs: This is a nice Chuck Berry-style intro lick that begins with a triplet-strummed D+ chord. Notice that this is a moveable version of a D+ that's in inversion. And this brings up a good point about augmented chords: there are really only four of them. Augmented chords are **symmetrical** chords, which means their intervallic structure is the same whether you ascend or descend. In the case of augmented chords, it's just a never-ending stream of major 3rd intervals (four half steps). Because of this, any note in an augmented chord could be considered the root. Take D+, for example. The notes are D, F#, and A#. But if you look at F# augmented, you'll see that it's spelled F#–A#–D. If you look at Bb+ (same as A#), it's spelled Bb–D–F#: same three notes. This means there are really only four different augmented chords: C+ (same as E+ or G#+), Db+ (same as F+ or A+), D+ (same as F#+ or Bb+), and Eb+ (same as G+ or B+). Neat stuff!

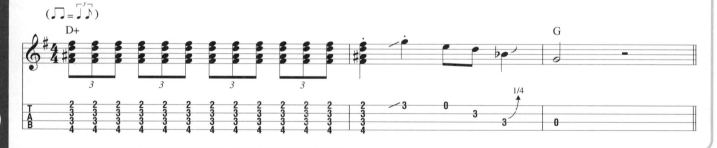

SUN

Miscellaneous: Let's add one more string to the tremolo technique here. When tremolo picking three or four strings, I prefer to use my index finger. You can certainly still use your thumb, but I find it easier to use my index. With an index-finger tremolo, I don't anchor my fingers on the uke; I keep them free. The motion involves wiggling the (mostly straight) index finger back and forth by rotating the wrist. You'll need to experiment with the angle of the index finger and how it contacts the strings to find the best motion for you. You're going for a smooth, feathered effect.

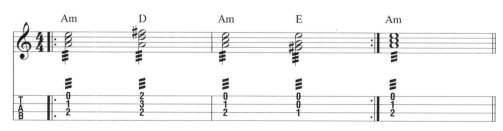

MON

Chord Vocabulary: We mentioned earlier in the book that any sus4 chord could be renamed as a sus2 chord with another root. This week, we'll take a closer look at that phenomenon and how it works. The basic formula is this: If you have a sus4 chord, it could also be named a sus2 chord with a root that's a 4th higher. So, Esus4 contains the same notes as Asus2—A is a 4th higher than E. Gsus4 contains the same notes as Csus2—C is a 4th higher than G. Play through each one of these chords and resolve each to the major triad shown in the top row first. In other words, play Esus4 and then play E. Play Gsus4 and then play G, etc. After you do that, do the same but with the bottom row of chord symbols: play Asus2 and then play A, play Csus2 and then play C, etc. You'll find that they work just as well resolving to either.

Esus4	Gsus4	Asus4	Dsus4	Csus4
Asus2	Csus2	Dsus2	Gsus2	Fsus2

TUE

Strumming: Let's put this sus chord duality at work in a triplet strumming pattern. Notice that the exact same chord is named differently depending on its function. In measure 1, the first chord is named Csus2 because it resolves to C. But in measure 2, the exact same chord is named Gsus4 because it resolves to G. Regarding the strumming hand, there are two possibilities: alternate down/up strums throughout, or down/up/down, down/up/down, etc. The faster the tempo, the more likely it is that you'll want to alternate strum direction throughout, but the latter method is very useful at slower to moderate tempos.

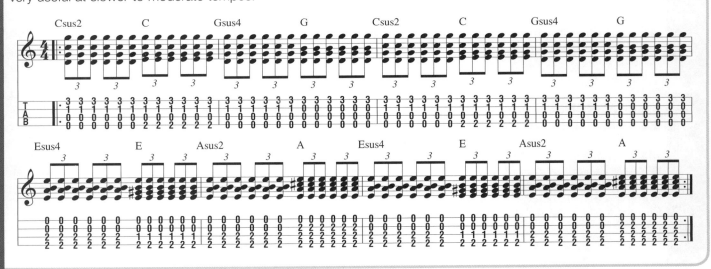

WED

Fingerstyle: We're looking at a new fingerpicking pattern here that's a modification of the popular Travis-picking pattern used by so many guitarists. Pay close attention to the plucking-hand indications between the staves. Your index and middle fingers remain on strings 2 and 1, respectively, while your thumb alternates between strings 4 and 3. And again, we demonstrate the yin and yang relationship of sus2 and sus4 chords.

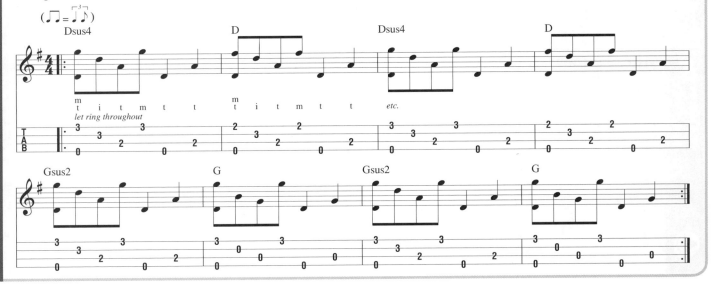

THU

Scale Exercise: We're using the full G major scale here and descending through an eight-note sequence that begins each time one scale degree lower. Try this one with both the alternating thumb technique and by alternating the i and m fingers to see which feels better to you.

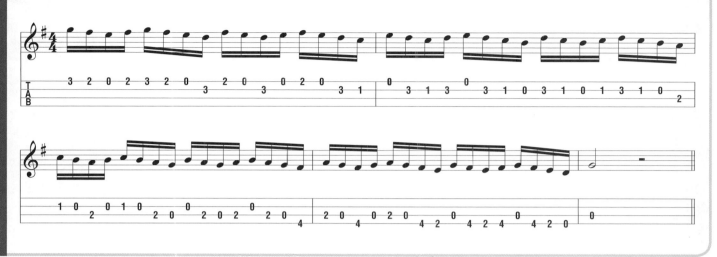

FRI

Legato: Here's another oblique motion exercise, but we're concentrating on sustaining a higher note while performing legato moves on a lower string. For measure 1, fret the high G note on string 1 with your pinky and hammer from the open string through to fret 3 with your index, middle, and ring fingers. For measure 4, use your ring finger for the D note on string 2 and your middle and index fingers for the legato moves on string 3.

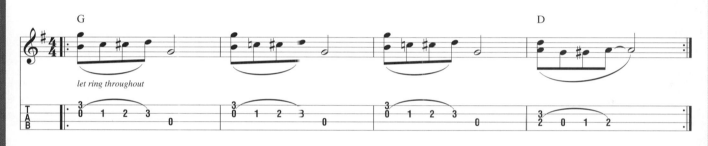

SAT

Licks & Riffs: This week is strictly for the fun of it. It's just a great-sounding blues riff in D minor that's fun to play. It doesn't really have anything to do with what we've worked on this week, but I figured you were due for some free time. Enjoy!

SUN

Miscellaneous: Finally, we reach the four-string tremolo this week. Again, I use my index finger for this, but you can try your thumb as well. Make sure all four strings are speaking out.

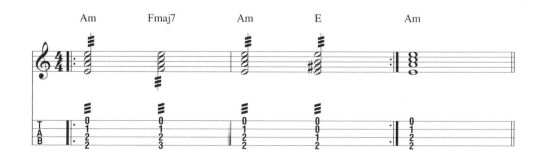

MON

Chord Vocabulary: This week we'll take a look at the **diminished triad**. This isn't a very common chord in pop music, but it does pop up on occasion. They're not the easiest chords to play as full, four-string chords, either, so we often mute a string and play only three. First we have the open D° form (the "°" symbol stands for "diminished"), which isn't too bad. However, if you try to play the moveable version shown as E°, you'll see that it's not terribly comfortable. Therefore, we can simply mute the fourth string of our open D° form (by allowing our barred index finger to touch it) and create a moveable form out of that. Next is an open F° form, which is very impractical as a moveable form, so we'll again mute the fourth string when playing the moveable version, shown here as F#°. Lastly, we have an open G#°. If you were to play this as a moveable form, it's quite a stretch on the lower frets, so we can just mute the first string on the moveable version, which is shown as A°. I fret this chord with the index on string 4, ring on string 3, and middle on string 2. The A° is actually one of the harder moveable versions of this chord because it's not very easy to mute the first string when you're that close to the nut. If you move up a half step to B♭°, for example, it's easier for the underside of your index finger to lay flat and mute the first string.

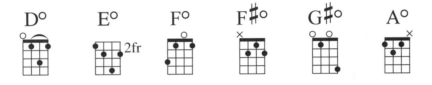

TUE

Strumming: We'll put our D° chord to work with this strumming exercise. Diminished chords are often used as passing harmonies between two other chords, as demonstrated here. Note that the notes on strings 1 and 3 descend chromatically through measures 1–3. In measure 3, we have an alternate version of the Em7 we saw in Week 5, now with a doubled D note instead of the open B string. This was done to maintain the descending pattern. And diminished chords have raised another good point with regards to muting strings: we don't always have to play the full, four-string versions of a triad. The D chord in measure 4, for example, is the moveable C-form chord from Week 10; we've just left off the note on string 1 to preserve the descending "melody" on top: F#–F–E–D. Keep the chords on beats 1 and 2 staccato, and be sure to mute the strings on beat 4 in measures 2 and 4 for the rest.

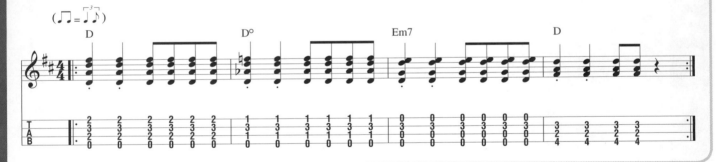

WED

Fingerstyle: Another common application for a diminished chord is to simply alternate it with a major triad of the same root. We'll do that here with a fingerpicking pattern that's a slight variation of last week's example. This week, we've simply moved the m and i fingers over a string set, which means our thumb will remain on string 4 throughout. Regarding the fingering for A°, this is a good example of when I would change the fingering to suit the context. While I'd normally fret the A° with index/ring/middle (low to high), here I'm using an index-finger barre on strings 4–2 and the middle finger on string 3 because I need to use an index-finger barre in measure 3 to reach the high A note on string 1 that follows in measure 4.

THU

Scale Exercise: This week we'll look at the concept of the **pivot note**. This is a repeated note that's alternated against a moving line. In this case, we're descending down the G major scale and using the high G as a pivot note. For a phrase such as this, I usually use a specific plucking-hand technique. In this case, I'm alternating the thumb (for the descending line) with a finger (for the pivot note). I've shown two options: t and i, or t and m. I tend to use t and m for this type of thing, possibly because I like the way it feels once the thumb starts to descend through the strings— i.e., it feels more natural than stretching my index finger over to string 1. But either way is perfectly doable, and you should try both to see what feels more comfortable.

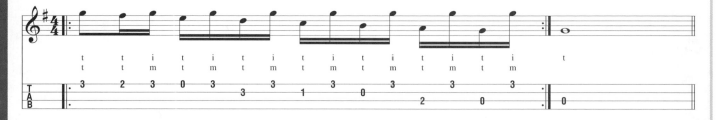

FRI

Legato: This is a classical-sounding example using more oblique motion. We have several hammer-ons and pull-offs strung together in the treble voice against single bass notes below. You'll need to barre fret 2 for the A chord on beat 3 of measure 1. Also take care in measure 2 not to bump string 3 while you're hammering and pulling on string 2. With regard to the plucking hand, there are lots of options here, but generally speaking, I'd suggest plucking the bass notes with the thumb and the treble melody with the fingers.

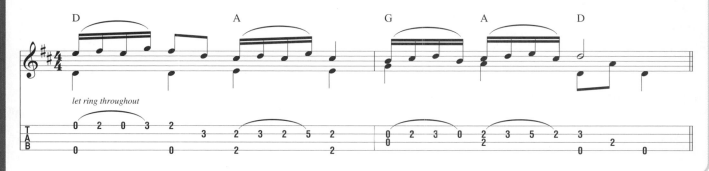

SAT

Licks & Riffs: Here's a fun riff in D that seems a bit all over the place at first, but when you break it down, it's not that difficult. It uses a **swung 16ths** feel. This is similar to the swung eighths feel, but the eighth notes are straight while the 16ths are swung. Listen to the audio to get a feel for this. Slide into the B note (fret 4, string 3) with your middle finger; remain here in third position through beat 3. At beat 4, shift down to first position for the D° chord arpeggio. You can either play this by barring with the index finger (if you'd like the notes to ring together) or playing the notes separately. As far as the plucking hand goes, just experiment to see what feels best; just about anything goes. I've added plucking suggestions between the staves, but this is by no means the only method.

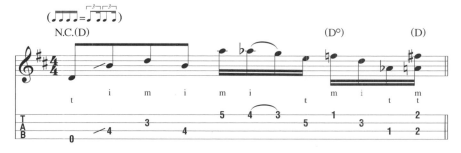

SUN

Miscellaneous: This week let's take a look at a concept called the **drone**. This involves maintaining a common note—it could be a bass note or treble note—against others changing above or below it. In our case, the open E string is acting as a drone in this bluesy lick in E. Be sure to keep your fret-hand fingers arched on string 2 so that string 1 can ring out fully. For the plucking hand, I use my m finger on string 1 throughout and my thumb for the descending line below it.

MON

Chord Vocabulary: Similar to the augmented triad, the **diminished 7th** chord—sometimes called a fully diminished chord—is a symmetrical chord consisting of stacked minor 3rd intervals. As such, there are really only three different diminished 7th chords: C°7, C#°7, and D°7. All others are simply inversions of one of these. Eb°7 contains the same notes as C°7, and E°7 contains the same notes as C#°7, etc. The open D°7 form is seen in its moveable form as E°7—far and away the most common fingering for this chord. In fact, the only other possibility is an open G°7. Its moveable form, shown here as A°7 in second position, is quite a stretch and definitely not something you'd casually grab!

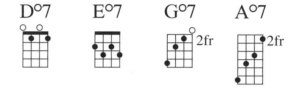

TUE

Strumming: Similar to diminished triads, fully diminished chords are great for use as passing chords, as demonstrated here with this example in F. We move from F to Gm, but with an F#°7 chord in between. These chords also do double duty as altered dominant chords. We'll look more at these chords later, but for now realize that the E°7 chord is functioning as a C dominant chord that's been altered to create some tension. (Compare this chord to the moveable C7 chord from Week 6, and you'll see that there's only one note that's different.) As such, this chord could also be called a rootless C7b9. The strum pattern here is rhythmically very active and involves staccato chords, rests, and muted strums (shown as X notes in the tab). For these muted strums, place your fingers on the strings, as if to fret the next chord, but don't push them down to the fretboard. You just want to deaden them so they produce a percussive "click" sound when you strum.

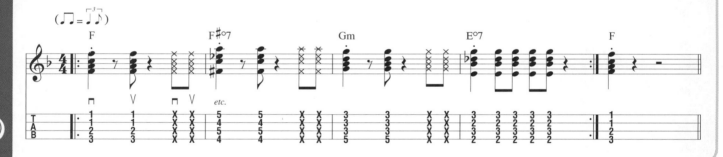

WED

Fingerstyle: We're applying the diminished 7th chord in similar ways here in the key of E, with F°7 and D#°7 chords. The fingerpicking pattern is another variation on the one we've been working with for the past few weeks, but this one involves the thumb and all three fingers. Remember also that, since you're only playing the notes on strings 4 and 1 at first, you don't need to fret the entire chord on the downbeat; you just need to have strings 4 and 1 covered. This is especially handy on the diminished 7th chords, which may not fall under the fingers as quickly as the others right away.

THU

Scale Exercise: This is basically the ascending version of last week's exercise. Since we want to work the lower strings, we're using the D major scale. Again, I use the m and t fingers for this, but try both ways for yourself.

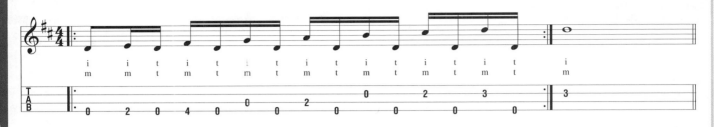

FRI

Legato: We'll return to single notes this week for some more involved legato moves. In this example, we're playing five notes with only one pluck. Your fret hand should remain in second position throughout; use the index finger for all notes on fret 2, middle for all notes on fret 3, etc. Notice the unusual slur marking at the end of measure 2 for the D note on string 2, fret 3. This is called a "hammer-on from nowhere," and it tells you to simply sound the note by hammering onto it. In other words, just imagine that note as another in the stream that began with the pluck on beat 3. As you hammer onto that final D note, allow your middle finger to nudge string 1 in the process, as this will prevent the open string from ringing out—something we *don't* want in this case.

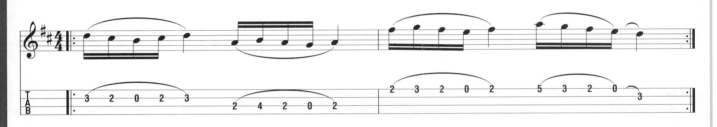

SAT

Licks & Riffs: To illustrate the symmetrical nature of diminished 7th chords, here's a Gypsy jazz-sounding riff in B minor. Note how the E°7 chord at the beginning is simply moved up in minor 3rds (three frets) before resolving to a Bm barre chord in seventh position. As such, all three of these diminished 7th chords are basically acting like inversions of an A#°7.

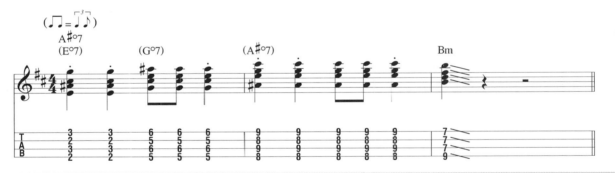

SUN

Miscellaneous: Here's another application of the drone technique using the open E string. By moving around chord shapes in the key of A minor and leaving the first string open, we create some nice, colorful chords. Measure 1 is the standard open A minor chord, and this form is moved up to what would normally be fifth position for a Dm chord. With the first string unfretted, though, we get a dense Dm(add9) chord. Next we have an E-form G chord in third position, which becomes G6 with the added open E string. And we finish with Am again. Other strings can be used as drones in this way as well, which we'll look at later.

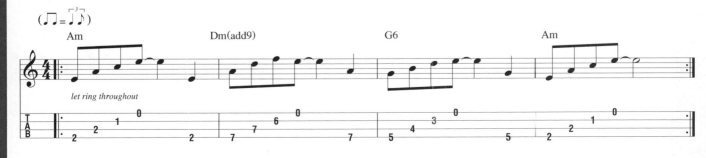

MON

Chord Vocabulary: This week we'll take a look at another new chord called the minor major 7th. This is like a minor 7th chord but with a natural 7th instead of a flat 7th. It's a pretty eerie chord on its own, but it's commonly used in certain progressions. The open Dm(maj7) form makes a usable moveable form, shown here as Em(maj7). The open Em(maj7) form sounds pretty funky out of context, but it—and its moveable form shown as F#m(maj7)—does have its uses, as we'll see. The open Fm(maj7) is uncomfortable enough, but the moveable form, shown as Gm(maj7), isn't fun at all. As such, it's definitely the least common.

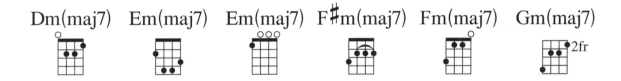

TUE

Strumming: Here's a strumming pattern in D minor to demonstrate the typical usage of the m(maj7) chord: as a passing harmony between a minor triad and a minor 7th chord of the same root. This creates a chromatic motion that's often continued one more half step, as it is here, to a m6 chord. I play this by plucking and strumming with the thumb throughout. You want to make sure that only the bass note is sounded on beat 1, so use a rest stroke with your thumb on those beats (see Week 14 for more on this).

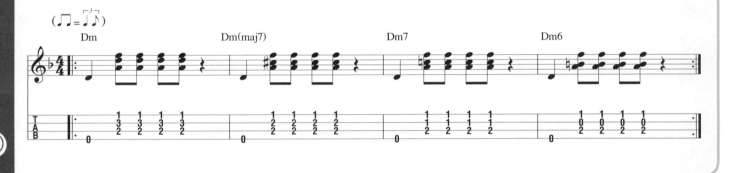

WED

Fingerstyle: Here's the same passing chord idea as in yesterday's example, this time applied to a fingerpicking riff in F minor. The idea here is to bring out a melody of sorts in the picking pattern. If we look at beat 1, we have a t-i-t-m pattern, in which the thumb moves from string 4 to string 3. This is a very common pattern, especially on guitar, and we could have easily repeated it throughout. However, I wanted to set apart the high F note on string 1, so I altered the pattern on beat 2 to avoid that note. This way, it sustains longer than any other note in the pattern, which helps to make the pattern sing a bit. Also notice the pause at the end of each measure—another common technique for keeping things fresh and interesting.

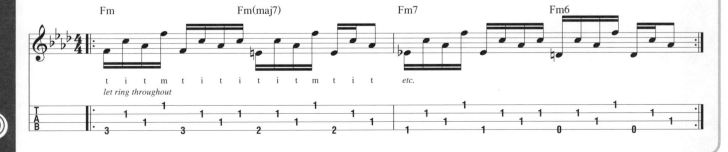

THU

Scale Exercise: This week we're using a sequence with the G major scale that ascends in three-note groups while moving down through each note of the scale. You may have to experiment with the fret-hand fingering in the first few beats, as you can get finger-tied a bit if you're not prepared for what's next. Try this one with alternating i and m fingers or alternating your thumb.

FRI

Legato: This exercise is all about precision and timing. We're alternating a two-note sequence (open string and fretted note) in a triplet rhythm, so you'll need to be very cognizant of your timing on this one. It's also critical to time the plucked notes on beat 3, measure 1 and beat 1, measure 2 properly. Try to keep the legato notes even in volume with an accent on the downbeats.

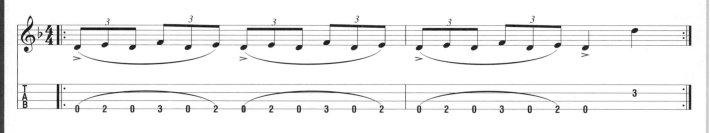

SAT

Licks & Riffs: Here's a beautiful fingerstyle riff in D minor that makes use of our open Dm(maj7) chord in a different way from the previous examples of this week. The great thing about this riff is that you really get a sense of two things going on at once: chords below and melody on top. To this end, pay close attention to the "*let ring*" indications in the music. Use your middle, ring, and index fingers (low to high) for the Dm(maj7) chord and play the following F note (fret 1, string 1) with your index and the G note (fret 3) with your pinky. You should still be holding down strings 3 and 2 up to this point. Then, shift up two frets to grab the A note with the pinky at fret 5 (you can let go of the chord now) and use your middle and index fingers for strings 3 and 2, respectively, in the Dm6 chord. Remember to sustain the high A note through beat 1 of measure 2. Finally, for the B♭maj7 chord, barre your index finger at fret 3 on strings 3–1 and use your pinky for the A note (fret 5, string 1) followed by your barred index finger for the G note (fret 3). It's a little complicated, but the result is worth it!

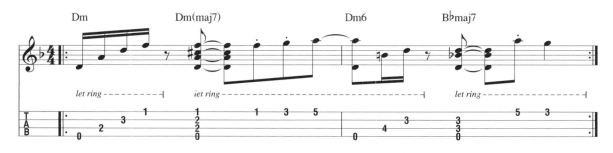

SUN

Miscellaneous: Here's another droning idea, this time using the open D string as a bass drone. We're moving the same triangular shape (strings 3–1 of the open D chord) up the fretboard to create different harmonies above the D bass note. The chord symbols with slashes in them (E/D, etc.) are called **slash chords**, and they indicate that a triad is played with an alternate bass note. "E/D," for example, is to be read as "E over D."

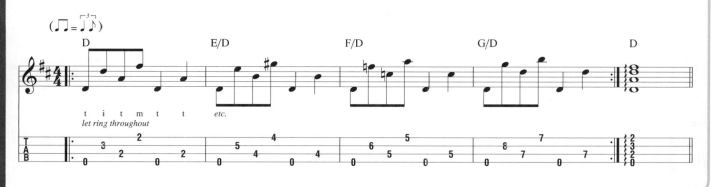

MON

Chord Vocabulary: This week we'll look at the dominant 9th chord, which is known as an **extended chord**. Since 9th chords technically contain five different notes—root, 3rd, 5th, ♭7th, and 9th—we have to omit one of them. This is usually the 5th, but not always, as we'll see in Week 25. We first have the open E♭9 followed by its moveable version as E9. Next is an open G9, which is very similar to the second version of G7 in Week 4. Its moveable version, shown as A9 in second position, is a bit of a stretch, but not too bad. Next is an open, rootless B♭9, which could also be called Dm7♭5 (see Week 12), shown in moveable form as C9. Finally, we have the open E9, which you can compare to the open E7 from Week 5. Since the root, E, has been replaced with the 9th, F♯, this is another rootless voicing, and this one in particular also goes by the name of G♯m7♭5 (Week 12). Use an index-finger barre to play the moveable version, shown as F9.

E♭9   E9   G9   A9   B♭9   C9   E9   F9

TUE

Strumming: We'll put the 9th chord to good use in a typical blues riff that includes the technique known as **stop-time**. In measures 1 and 2, strum the triplets using your thumb or index finger in alternate strokes and stop on a dime for beat 3, quickly muting the strings afterward. In measure 3, strum steady triplets while gradually increasing in volume until you get to measure 4. At that point, maintain the triplet rhythm but accent each downbeat with a harder strum. This riff would be followed by moving to the IV chord—D7 in this case.

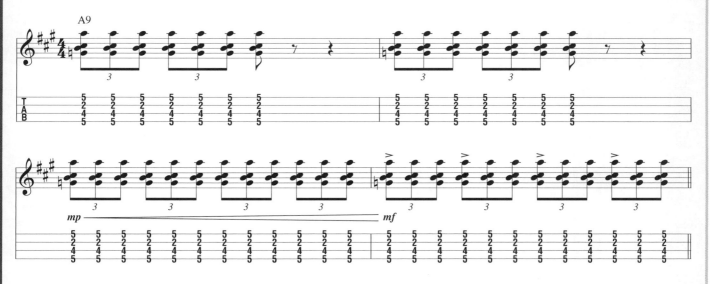

WED

Fingerstyle: Your r finger will get a good workout with this rolling triplet pattern. The A6 chord is a bit of a squeeze since you'll (most likely) be fretting the A chord with three fingers, but it's doable. Once you get the fingerpicking pattern down, try injecting some dynamics into it. In other words, try swelling in volume a bit as you approach the F♯ note on string 1, fret 2 and backing down a bit afterward.

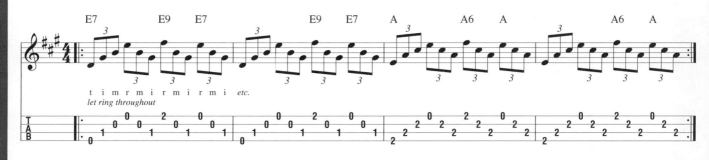

Scale Exercise: This week's exercise is essentially a reverse of last week's. This time we're ascending through the G major scale with descending three-note groups. There are a few instances, like when moving from the last note of beat 1, measure 1 to beat 2, measure 1, where you'll need to roll a fret-hand finger from one string to the other. In this first instance, it will be either your index finger (if you begin in second position) or your middle finger (if you begin in first position). The exercise also presents challenges for your plucking hand, as you'll need to skip from string 4 to string 2 halfway through measure 1.

Legato: This week we continue with the idea from last week, in which we're mixing up plucked and legato notes in a more unpredictable manner. You're not always plucking on the down beats here, so it's up to your fret hand to really keep the notes steady in rhythm.

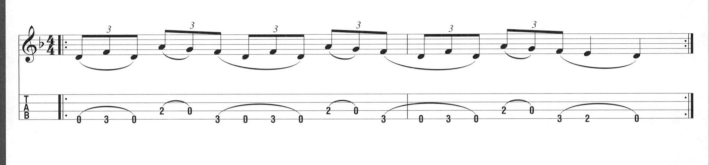

Licks & Riffs: Here's a fun jazzy turnaround chord sequence that will test your chordal knowledge. After we run chromatically down with dominant 9th chords, we wrap it up with two chords from earlier weeks—Am7 and F#°7 (functioning as D7♭9)—before resolving to a G chord. Keep the chords staccato!

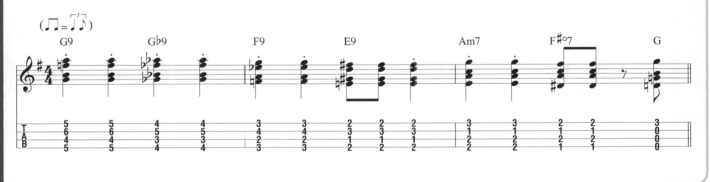

Miscellaneous: This week we'll use the open B and E strings as drones while moving through various E-form chords (fretting only the two bottom strings). The resulting harmonies are lush and beautiful. Use fingerpicking on this one with your thumb and three fingers assigned to one string each throughout.

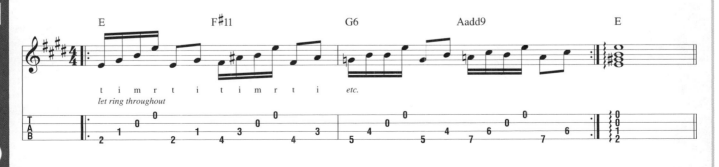

MON

Chord Vocabulary: Now we'll take a look at minor 9th chords. First up is the open Em9 form and its moveable version shown as Fm9. This is a fairly common form. The open G#m9 form becomes quite a stretch when played in its moveable form (shown as Am9), but it is possible if you really want it. The second open G#m9 is a nice-sounding chord and, just like its dominant counterpart last week (G9), is rootless. The moveable form, shown as Am9, is a bit of a finger-twister, but it's certainly playable. These chords are actually a major 7th form that we haven't covered yet, so I've listed their alternate ego chord names in parentheses. Finally, we have Em9 and its moveable barre shape, Fm9. These are also rootless voicings, and you'll recognize the Em9 as Gmaj7 from Week 2. (Consequently, Fm9 could also be called Abmaj7.)

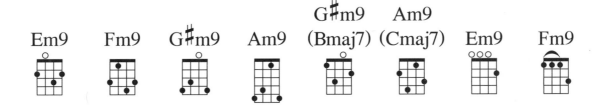

Em9   Fm9   G#m9   Am9   G#m9 (Bmaj7)   Am9 (Cmaj7)   Em9   Fm9

TUE

Strumming: Here's a nice, syncopated strum pattern using our Em9 chord that includes lots of rests and sustained chords. The accents are almost all on the upbeats here, and in fact you're starting with an upstroke because of the rest on the first eighth note. Be sure to count and tap your foot at first to make sure you're not rushing anywhere. I like to strum this one with my thumb, but you can use the index if you'd like.

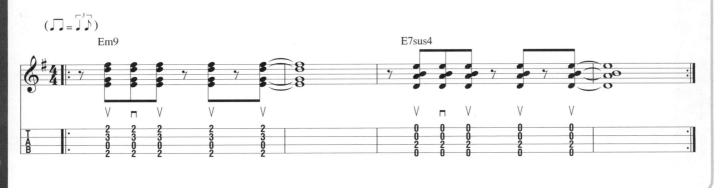

WED

Fingerstyle: This is a beautiful fingerpicking example that incorporates our open G#m9 chord. There are just about endless variations on these alternating thumb patterns. The key here is timing and patience. Make sure you give each quarter note its full duration. Just imagine that you're watching flowers slowly blooming in a backyard garden.

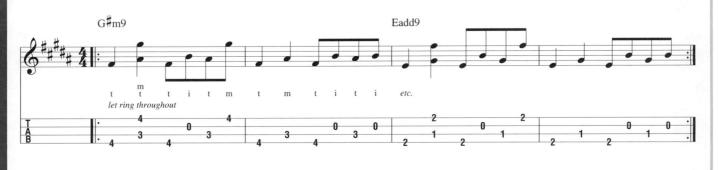

THU

Scale Exercise: Continuing on with our sequence ideas in G major, here's a four-note sequence that descends through the scale. This makes an excellent exercise whether you alternate plucking fingers or use alternating thumb strokes. Remember to tap your foot as you play to keep the tempo steady!

FRI

Legato: We're continuing to work with legato notes bleeding over accented beats this week with another riff in D minor. (Actually, the B♮ note in measure 4 makes this a D **Dorian** riff.) Aside from the first note of each measure, none of the plucked notes here appear on the beat. This means you really need to keep your legato notes steady and always be mindful of where the beat is so that you don't lose your place. Measure 4 is particularly difficult to keep from sounding lopsided. You want the accents to fall on the beats—not only on the plucked notes. So in beat 1, for example, you'll want to pluck the A note on string 3, fret 2 a little quieter than normal and pull off to the open G string (which falls on the beat) a bit harder than normal to place the accent where it should be.

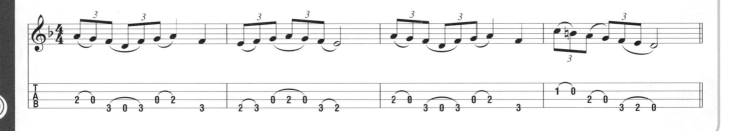

SAT

Licks & Riffs: This week we make use of the moveable Fm9 chord in a jazzy blues line. You can play the chord by strumming it or plucking it fingerstyle; either way has its own charm. For the descending line in measure 2, which is straight down the F blues scale, I tend to use my m finger for string 1 and pluck everything else with the thumb. But there are plenty of other options that would work. Regarding the fret hand, I like to shift a bit to grab fret 4, string 3 with my ring finger so that I can then slide it down one fret and pull off to the index finger on fret 1. You could also use your pinky here for fret 4 and slide it down; it just means you'll have to collapse your hand position a little when pulling off from your pinky to your index finger.

SUN

Miscellaneous: More fun with drone strings ensues this week with an interesting three-chord progression created from using only the three lower strings of E-form chords. The high E string is allowed to ring open throughout, creating the colorful harmonies of Fmaj7, G6, and F♯m7. The fingering for the latter is a bit tricky. I like to use pinky, index, middle (low to high), but you might find something else that feels better. There's almost no end to this kind of experimentation.

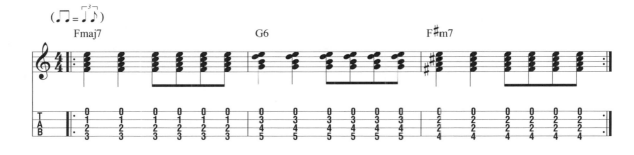

MON

Chord Vocabulary: Let's take this week to play catch up and cover some chords or forms that have slipped by the wayside thus far. First up is a moveable maj7 form shown here as Gmaj7 in second position. This is derived from the open Fmaj7 chord in Week 8. Next we have a moveable E♭maj7 based on the open Dmaj7 chord also from Week 8. The open E7 chord is an alternate version that omits the 5th of the chord, B. However, it's a great-sounding chord that's very useful. The moveable version of this chord is shown as F7 in first position. It's not terribly comfortable in its moveable form, but it's doable; remember to keep the thumb behind the neck. Fm7 is the moveable version of the Em7 chord shown in Week 7. This one requires an index-finger barre.

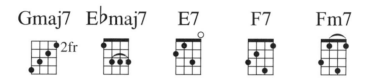

TUE

Strumming: We're putting two different moveable major 7th forms to work with this strumming exercise. Be sure to follow the strum directions here; your strumming hand should be moving with the beat steadily throughout, even when you're resting or sustaining a chord, as this will help you stay in time.

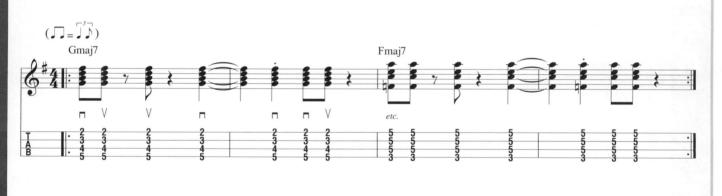

WED

Fingerstyle: Here's a swampy-sounding riff with our alternate open E7 chord that may sound a little familiar to some of you. It's syncopated throughout, so be careful of your timing. Note the plucking-hand directions. Although you could play this riff using t, i, m, and r, I'd like you to use only t, i, and m, smoothly pushing your thumb through strings 4 and 3.

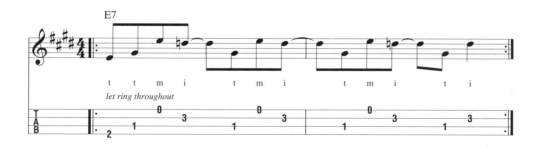

Scale Exercise: This is the opposite of last week's sequence. We're moving up through the G major scale with a four-note sequence.

Legato: It's not easy at all to make this exercise sound properly accented—i.e., on the beats. If you're not careful, the plucked notes will end up sounding accented by default, and the timing will likely suffer. We're climbing triplets with two notes per string, which means that, aside from the first note in each pattern, the plucked notes are not going to appear on the beat. At the end of measure 2, we have a "hammer-on from nowhere" on string 4. This helps set up the repeat of the exercise, as it prevents you from having to pick two notes in a row on string 4. Take this one slowly at first and really concentrate on the timing and accents, which should generally always fall on the beat unless otherwise indicated.

Licks & Riffs: This jazzy line makes a great ending lick in G major. After playing the first Gmaj7 chord—the moveable form of the open Dmaj7—slide indistinctly down a few frets while releasing the fret-hand pressure. The next line is a little tricky, so let's go through the fingering closely. After the open B string and the C note at fret 1 (played with the index), hammer on to fret 2 with your middle finger and then slide it up to fret 3. This will place you in second position for the start of measure 2, which allows you to grab the F♯ note on string 1, fret 2 with your index. On beat 2 of measure 2, you have two options: you can remain in second position and use your pinky for fret 5 and your middle finger for the fret 3 pull-offs, or you can shift up to third position and grab fret 5 with your ring finger, using the index finger for the fret 3 pull-offs. Ideally, you should be able to handle both, but one way will most likely feel better to you. I strum the first chord with my thumb and pluck the remaining notes with a combination of thumb and fingers.

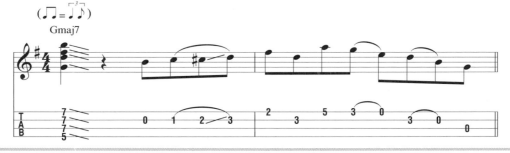

Miscellaneous: Who says you can't have three droning strings? Granted, this kind of restricts your key options, but you can create some really nice riffs with this idea. Here we're moving notes along string 4 while keeping the top three strings open to craft a memorable phrase in E minor. The plucking hand should adhere to a one-finger-per-string approach throughout (thumb on string 4, index on string 3, etc.), and be careful of the slight syncopation at the end of beat 2. Listen to the audio if you're having trouble making out the rhythm.

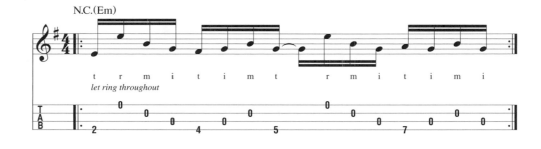

WEEK 23

MON

Chord Vocabulary: We'll continue playing catch-up this week by checking out some chord forms that we've missed. The first, A5, is the moveable version of G5 from Week 3 and requires a double barre: index finger and pinky. The E5 shows an open version of a "power chord" that requires you to mute string 3. This is done by allowing your middle finger (or whichever finger you're using to fret the E note on string 4) to touch string 3 while fretting string 4. This is shown in moveable form as F5, which requires an index-finger barre on strings 2–1. It's even easier to mute string 3 in this chord because you can either use the underside of your ring finger (on string 4) or the tip of your index finger (barring strings 2–1). The next E5 is the moveable form of D5 from Week 3. Allow the underside of your pinky (fretting string 2) to touch string 1 to keep it quiet. A7 is the moveable form of the second G7 in Week 4 and requires a bit of a stretch. Use the ring finger on string 4, an index-finger barre for strings 3–2, and the pinky for string 1. Finally, the Asus4 is the moveable form of Gsus4 in Week 3.

A5   E5   F5   E5   A7   Asus4

TUE

Strumming: It's time to rock out with some power chords. We're using all three power chord forms here. I like to strum this one with my index finger because it sounds a little more aggressive, which suits the style. Tap your foot along to the beat and watch the rhythm in measure 2, because it gets a little syncopated.

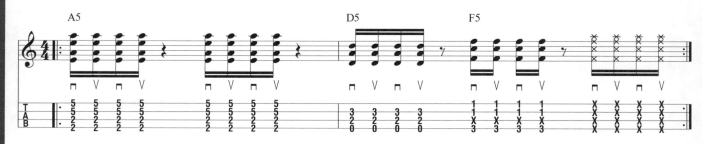

WED

Fingerstyle: We'll put our moveable Asus4 and A7 chords to work here with a nice-sounding pattern that uses a banjo roll technique. We're playing a three-note pattern of t-i-m in continuous eighth notes, which creates syncopation. We turn the pattern around at the end of each measure by playing only two notes: 3 + 3 + 2 = 8. Since the root of these chords (A) lies on string 3, we're starting the thumb on that string and alternating strings 3–4–3, 3–4–3, etc. Your index finger may get tired of holding the barre all day, so be sure to take a rest if you need to!

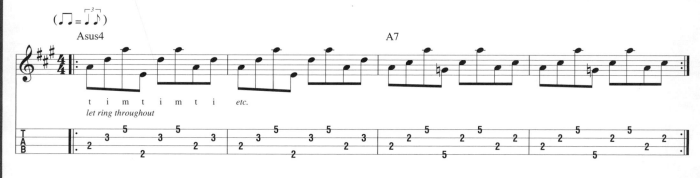

THU

Scale Exercise: This week we're going to start working on position playing, which means we'll move up the fretboard a bit and won't be using any open strings. This is an A major scale that's basically a moveable form of the open G major scale we've been using so much thus far. The main difference is that we're able to access the 7th note below the root on string 3, whereas when playing the open G major scale, we had to access this note (F#, in that case) on string 4. You should remain in second position when descending strings 1 and 2, but when you reach string 3, shift down to first position (pinky on fret 4, middle on fret 2, index on fret 1) temporarily. When you come back up, shift back to second position once you hit string 2. This isn't terribly different from what we've been doing, but your fret-hand is now working just as hard as your plucking hand, so be sure the two stay in sync.

FRI

Legato: This is the same scale exercise as yesterday, but now we're playing legato throughout. Again, the plucked notes are not falling on the beats, so be very aware of your tempo. There's a tendency for many people to rush through hammer-ons and pull-offs, and if you do that here, it's going to stick out like a sore thumb. This is great practice for your pinky too; you really have to whack those hammer-ons to get them to sound clearly!

SAT

Licks & Riffs: This is just a fun fingerstyle riff in A that uses parallel dominant 7th voicings: A7 and G7. If it weren't for the high A note on string 1, you could get away with playing this whole thing in second position. But, alas, you'll need to stretch on the A7 chord a bit so you can use the pinky for the high A note. Although, you could play measure 1 in second position if you'd like.

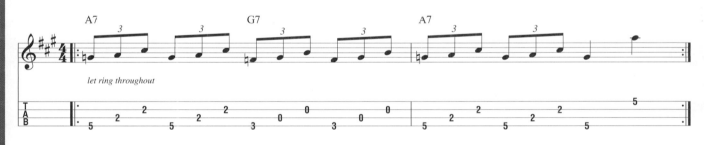

SUN

Miscellaneous: Let's hear an example in E minor using the middle two strings as drones. We'll move parallel 9th (octave plus a 2nd) intervals on strings 4 and 1 to different spots along the scale to generate some nice harmonies. The fingerpicking is a standard alternating thumb pattern, and the open G string on beat 4 of each measure will give you plenty of time for the position shifts.

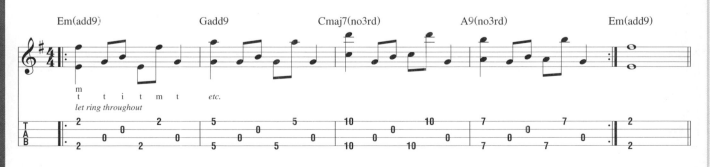

MON

Chord Vocabulary: Let's look at just a few more chord forms we've overlooked so far, and next week we'll get back to new types. The first chord, E, is the moveable form of the open D chord from Week 1. It's not a terribly comfortable chord to play, but it's certainly usable in certain situations. The following Em is the moveable form of Dm from Week 4 and is a bit easier than its major counterpart. Next we have Esus4, which is the moveable version of Dsus4 (Week 3), and E7sus4, which is the moveable version of D7sus4 (Week 4). Finally, Em7 is the moveable version of Dm7 from Week 5. It can be played using all four fingers, but some people prefer to use the index on string 4, ring on string 3, and the barred middle finger for strings 2 and 1. Try both fingerings out to see what feels best to you.

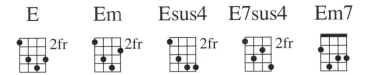

TUE

Strumming: We'll put our E7sus4 chord to work this week with a nifty little strum pattern that mixes thumb plucks with index-finger strums. Pay close attention to the indications between the staves. You first pluck string 4 with a downstroke of the thumb (use the flesh—not the nail). This is followed by three index-finger strums: up, down, up. It's a nice pattern because the thumb generally sounds a bit warmer than the index finger (at least for me it does), so you get a nice separation that almost sounds like two different instruments.

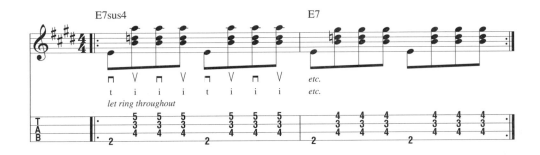

WED

Fingerstyle: Here's a beautiful fingerpicking pattern that applies the alternating thumb technique to triplets. The pattern is six triplets long and consists of t–i–t–m–t–i. Notice that you're not alternating steadily back and forth with the thumb; you're spending twice as much time on string 3 as you are string 4. You're also plucking with the i finger twice as much as with the m finger. Pay careful attention to the markings, and you'll get it. It feels a little different at first, but the result is a smooth, rolling pattern that seems to almost float with weightlessness.

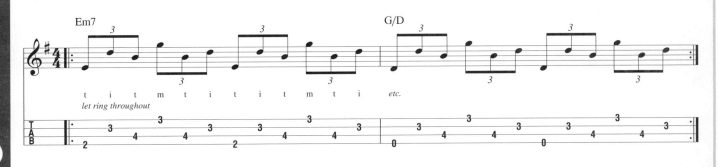

THU

Scale Exercise: Are you ready for this? We're taking the same A major scale we worked on last week, adding a few more notes below the tonic on string 4, and working a rigorous 3rds sequence down and up through the entire length. Again, though you'll spend most of your time in second position, you will need to shift down to first position for a bit at the bottom of the arc. When descending, I shift to first position on beat 4 of measure 1, with my pinky on fret 4, string 3. When ascending, I shift back to second position on the "and" of beat 2, measure 2, using my index finger to roll from fret 2, string 3 to fret 2, string 2. This is a lot of notes to play without stopping, so take your time to work up the fingering before trying to speed it up. Regarding the plucking hand, I usually alternate i and m fingers for this exercise. Depending on which plucking finger you start with, one direction will probably be easier for you. But it's all good practice!

FRI

Legato: Now let's try the 3rds sequence from yesterday but with legato techniques whenever possible. In other words, whenever there's more than one note on a string, we'll use hammer-ons and/or pull-offs. This may be a bit awkward at first because it's hard to keep track of where the legato moves will be. You may find yourself plucking a note when you don't have to because it lands on a strong beat, for example. But take it slowly at first and make sure that you're using legato whenever possible. This technique—i.e., mixing legato and plucked notes—results in a musical sound that naturally tends to have a nice ebb and flow to it.

SAT

Licks & Riffs: Here's a cool, Flamenco-sounding fingerpicking riff in Dm that uses the open high E string atop a B♭ chord to create a colorful B♭add#11 harmony. The B♭ and D notes on strings 3 and 2, respectively, are then slid down a half step to form an A major chord. Don't miss the slight alteration at the end of measure 4. Note that, although it's not written in the music, I'd usually **ritard** a bit (i.e., slow down) before playing the final Dm chord.

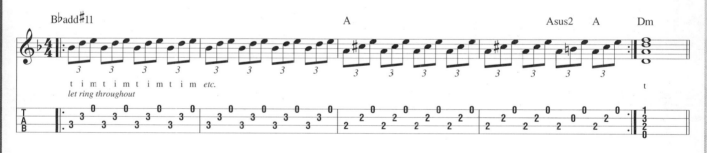

SUN

Miscellaneous: This week we'll start working again with **double stops** in a more deliberate fashion. We'll basically be harmonizing melodies, mostly in 3rd intervals, which last more than one or two notes. This example simply walks up and back down the first four notes of a C major scale on string 2—C, D, E, and F—while harmonizing a diatonic (i.e., in the key of C in this case) 3rd above each.

55

MON

Chord Vocabulary: Let's pick up where we left off in Week 21 with our study of 9th chords. This week we'll look at the major 9th chord, which is just like a dominant 9th but with a natural 7th instead of a flatted one. These are not easy to play on the uke, so some compromises have to be made at times. The first Ebmaj9 open chord is a true maj9 chord with a root, major 3rd, major 7th, and major 9th. The moveable form, shown as Emaj9, is not the most comfortable chord on the planet, but it can be played. The next chord, Dmaj9, doesn't contain a 3rd. Since the 3rd of the chord is what determines whether it's major or minor, this is not a true maj9 chord, but it still acts like one almost all of the time and sounds reminiscent of it. The moveable form, shown as Ebmaj9, requires an index-finger barre. The Fmaj9 chord also does not contain a 3rd, so it's not a true maj9 chord. In fact, since the 9th (G in this case) appears right above the root, you may hear some people refer to this chord as Fmaj7sus2, although this is not a standardized chord name. Another possible name for this chord is C/F, which means it's a C chord with an F bass note. Compare strings 1–3 with the open C chord, and you'll see what I mean. The moveable version of this chord, shown as Gmaj9, requires a bit of a stretch and an index-finger barre, but it's still plenty accessible.

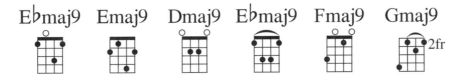

TUE

Strumming: We make use of both Ebmaj9 forms in this strumming exercise. This one is all about counting and keeping a steady tempo. There aren't a lot of strums here; they're spread out a bit and slightly syncopated. So you need to be sure you're tapping your foot and/or counting along so you know where you are in the measure. I've added strum direction markings that coincide with keeping your strumming hand moving in straight eighth notes. Keep the hand moving down on the downbeats and only make contact with the strings at the appropriate times.

WED

Fingerstyle: Here's a variation on last week's pattern. We're working the alternating thumb into a triplet phrase again, but instead of the thumb playing a pattern of string 4, string 3, string 3, as it did last week, here we're playing string 4, string 3, string 4 as the pattern. If you fret the Dsus2 chord with the index and middle finger, you can leave those two in place when moving to the Gmaj9 chord.

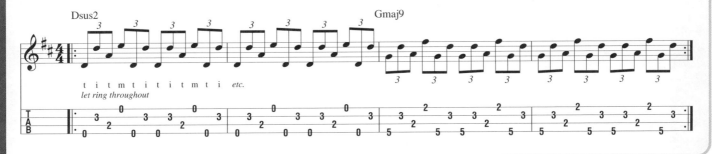

Scale Exercise: Here we're using the A minor pentatonic scale in second/third position with a cascading descending sequence that lasts two beats. It's repeated on each lower string set. There are several points at which you can either roll a finger from a fret to the same fret on an adjacent string, or use two different fingers. The end of beat 1 is a prime example. You should try both fingering methods to see which you prefer.

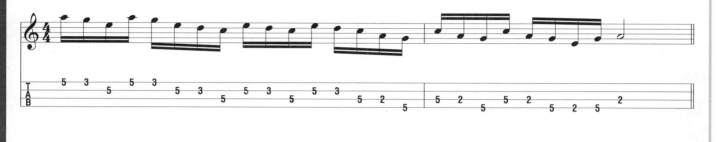

Legato: This is Thursday's scale exercise performed legato style. It's all pull-offs save for one combination pull-off/hammer-on at the end. Again, most of the pull-offs fall on weak beats, so concentrate on making this one sound steady and even.

Licks & Riffs: Here's a nice chordal riff that shows how you can dress up some basic chords. You could reduce the essence of this riff to simply F–C in each measure: F on beat 1 and C on beat 2.5. But we've changed the F to an Fmaj9(no 3rd) and added a little bass riff to create some movement. This technically creates other passing chords (C and D9sus4—see next week's Monday lesson for more on the 9sus4 chord), but the essence is still F to C. We also add a hammer-on ornament on beat 4 in measure 1. Notice that the 16th notes are swung in this riff. There aren't many, but listen to the audio if you're still not sure about how this sounds.

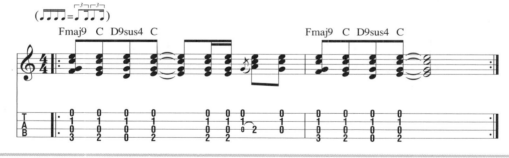

Miscellaneous: Let's expand a bit on the 3rds double stops we learned last week. We're using the same exact set here, but we've created a nice little melody with them. Aside from the first and last double stop, for which I use my index finger on string 2, I prefer to keep my ring finger on string 2 throughout, using either my index finger (two-fret spread) or middle finger (one-fret spread) on string 1. However, you could also keep your index finger on string 1 throughout and switch between your middle and ring fingers on string 2. It's up to you, as both will work equally well here.

MON

Chord Vocabulary: We'll break more new ground this week with another type of dominant chord called the 9sus4. This is just like the 9th chords we learned in Week 20, but the 3rd of the chord has been replaced with the 4th, just as in the sus4 triad and the 7sus4 chord. Again, as with the other 9th chords, we're forced to omit one of the five notes that technically make up this chord. And, again, it's usually the 5th. You'll find that, as we get further into extended chords, more and more chords pull double duty as others with alternate names. First up is D9sus4, which could also be called C/D. The moveable version, shown as E9sus4, requires a full index-finger barre. You may recognize F#9sus4 and the moveable G9sus4 as Eadd9 and Fadd9, respectively, from Week 8. Alternate the G9sus4 voicing here with the open G9 chord from Week 20, however, and you should be able to hear its dominant function. Next we have the open rootless G9sus4, which we already saw as Dm7 in Week 5. Compare this chord to the open G7sus4 in Week 13 to see how it differs. The moveable version as A9sus4 looks just like Em7 from Week 24. Finally, we have another rootless version, the open E9sus4, which you may recognize as D6 (Week 10) or, if you're really astute, Bm7. Compare this chord and its moveable form (shown as F9sus4) to the open E9 and moveable F9 in Week 20.

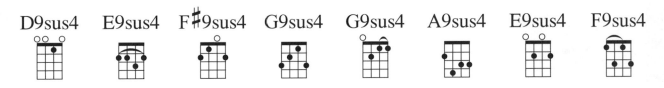

| D9sus4 | E9sus4 | F#9sus4 | G9sus4 | G9sus4 | A9sus4 | E9sus4 | F9sus4 |

TUE

Strumming: Let's put our new 9sus4 chords to work in another rhythmic strumming pattern that's heavily syncopated. Be sure to mute the strings on the rests by laying your strumming and/or fretting hand fingers onto the strings to quiet them. Your strumming hand should be moving in a steady rhythm throughout, with downstrokes paired with downbeats. Notice that the final chord here, labeled as Em7, was also labeled as A9sus4 yesterday. However, as mentioned previously, these chord shapes often pull double or triple duty, and context is the only way to determine the proper name. In this context, the chord functions more as an Em7.

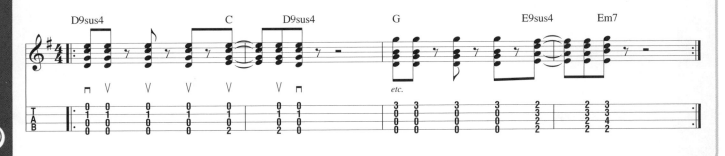

WED

Fingerstyle: Here's a rolling triplet pattern that changes direction halfway through. You want a very smooth sound here, so that means you may need to experiment with fret-hand fingerings to find ones that you can grab quickly and easily. Two of these chords could be analyzed with other names. G9sus4 could be called Fadd9, and that would fit in this context as well. However, since it was followed by G9, it made more sense to me to call it G9sus4. Eadd9 could also be called F#9sus4 (as shown in Monday's chord grids), but that didn't make as much sense in this context.

THU

Scale Exercise: This is basically the ascending version of last week's sequence. The very end is slightly different because we would have had to shift to a higher position in order to perfectly mirror the descending version. You'll need to remain in second position until beat 4 of measure 1. At that point, you can shift to third position to use your index finger on fret 3 if you'd prefer. At the end of beat 1, you'll need to roll your index finger from string 3, fret 2 to string 4, fret 2. In order to do this, fret string 3 using more of the pad of the finger instead of the tip. The same type of thing happens at fret 3 on strings 1 and 2, so be prepared for that.

FRI

Legato: And this is the legato version of yesterday's exercise, which uses mostly hammer-ons. Again, it's imperative that you maintain a steady tempo through the hammer-ons so the phrase doesn't sound lopsided.

SAT

Licks & Riffs: This is a nice, bluesy lick in A minor that makes use of the A blues scale in second/third position. This is just like the A minor pentatonic scale we've been using for Thursday's and Friday's lessons from the past two weeks, with the addition of one note: E♭ (or D♯), shown here at fret 4, string 2. I use my i and m fingers for plucking on this one throughout. Again, at the beginning of measure 2, you'll need to roll the index finger from string 3 to string 4.

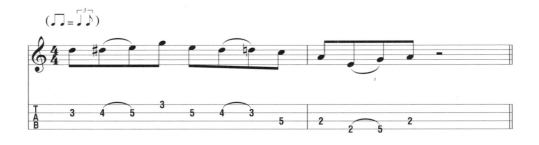

SUN

Miscellaneous: This week we'll take a look at more double stops in the key of C, but we'll move down to the other string sets as well. I'm plucking these simultaneously in a fingerstyle technique, but you could strum the two strings with your thumb or index finger as well for a different tone.

MON

Chord Vocabulary: Before we venture further into the extended and (eventually) altered world, let's backpedal a bit and look at some different ways to skin the cats with which we're already familiar: triads. Triads contain three different notes, yet most of the voicings we've learned thus far use all four strings, which means one of the notes was doubled in a different octave. Let's get a little more systematic with them, now, and play three-note chords without doubling any of the notes. There are two main categories in this regard: **open voicings** and **closed voicings**. Open voicings are those in which the notes of the chord span more than one octave; in closed voicings, they don't span more than one octave. Here are the major triad closed voicings on strings 4–2 shown in open and moveable form in three possible inversions: root position (root on bottom), first inversion (3rd on bottom), and second inversion (5th on bottom). You'll no doubt recognize all these as partial versions of chords we've already learned. With regards to the plucking hand, you may want to use fingerstyle for these chords so that you don't have to worry about muting the other string. Especially when we get into the open-voiced chords, this comes in handy.

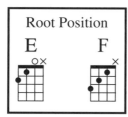
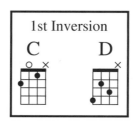
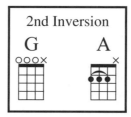

Root Position	1st Inversion	2nd Inversion
E F	C D	G A

TUE

Strumming: We'll put these new forms to work here with a rhythmic strumming pattern that's got some syncopation and rests mixed for dynamic effect. Be sure to quiet the strings during the rests for maximum impact.

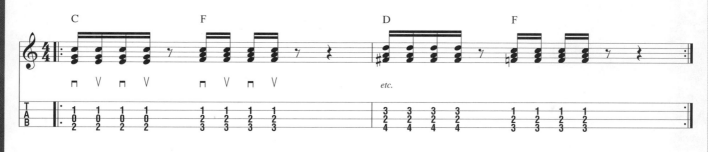

WED

Fingerstyle: We're using the block-chord fingerstyle approach here, with a few exceptions, to play a progression in D major. Notice that we're employing two different forms for the D and A chords. This is done to create a little melody in the treble voice. Throughout the riff, use t on string 4, i on string 3, and m on string 2.

THU

Scale Exercise: This is an excellent workout for both hands. We're using the A minor pentatonic scale in second/third position again and zigzagging down with an every-other-note sequence that moves in 4ths or 3rds. You'll have several fretting options throughout. I like to use a pinky-ring combination when moving from fret 5 on one string to fret 5 on the adjacent string. Regarding the plucking hand, I've added a suggestion between the staves, but you could also alternate thumb strokes.

FRI

Legato: In this exercise, we're using an E minor pentatonic scale in second/third position, but we're also including the open strings to create a four-note sequence on strings 4–2. For each of these, you'll have a pull-off/hammer/hammer move using two fretted notes and one open string. Pay close attention to the tab in this regard.

SAT

Licks & Riffs: We're using the same E minor pentatonic scale form from yesterday, minus the open strings, to create a truly moveable riff. By adding the ♭5th note (B♭ or A♯), we're technically playing the E blues scale. I begin this riff in third position, with the index finger on fret 3, string 1. In measure 2, after pulling off from fret 4 (middle finger) to fret 3 (index finger), slide the index down to fret 2 without picking it.

SUN

Miscellaneous: This time we're working through double stops from a G minor pentatonic scale in open position. I use my pinky and ring finger for all the third-fret notes, but you could also barre your ring finger if you'd like. Regarding the plucking hand, I find that, for slower riffs like this where speed isn't really a big factor, it works best for me if I just use the same plucking fingers throughout. For example, I may use my i and m fingers, working together in a locked method, with the index plucking the lowest-pitched string of each double stop and the middle finger plucking the highest-pitched.

MON

Chord Vocabulary: Let's continue with our closed voicings of major triads this week on strings 3–1. Again we'll have open and moveable forms of three different inversions.

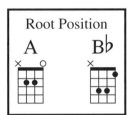
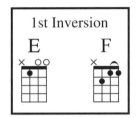
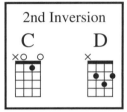

TUE

Strumming: This is a quick, snappy-sounding strum that uses all three of our forms from yesterday. It's mostly played with quick downstrokes (keep your hand moving on every beat), but don't miss the staccato strums in measure 2, as they're essential to the sound.

WED

Fingerstyle: Use a plucking pattern of m-i-t throughout this example, which moves down different triad forms in the key of D from seventh to open position. Concentrate on smoothness between chord transitions. This may mean only planting your first finger on string 1 at first so that the other notes of the previous chord can ring right up until the first note of the new chord. One way to accomplish this is to use an index-finger barre on strings 1–3 through the first two measures. Even though you don't need it for the D and C chords, it allows you to easily transition to the chords that follow.

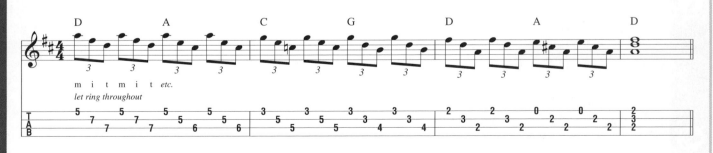

Scale Exercise: This week we're using the A Dorian mode in second position. This is just like an A minor scale, except it has a natural 6th degree instead of a flat one. I play this entire exercise in second position, rolling my pinky from fret 5, string 2 to fret 5, string 1 to repeat the phrase. If you play it this way, your fret-hand pinky will get some great practice. For the plucking, I either alternate thumb strokes or alternate the i and m fingers.

Legato: When performed with the same fret-hand fingering as Thursday's exercise, this one will really work out your pinky. Make sure all the notes are loud and clear and that your tempo remains steady.

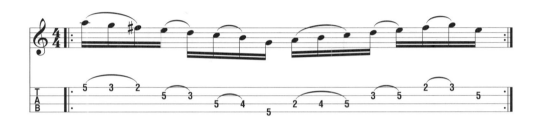

Licks & Riffs: Here's a great little riff in D that's kind of a question-and-answer format. The chordal riff of D–G is answered with a melodic riff from the D major pentatonic scale. This occurs three times (notice the "*play 3 times*" indication) before we wrap it up with a descending lick that includes the bluesy ♭3rd note (F). I've included my preferred fingering for the plucking hand, but feel free to try something different if you'd like.

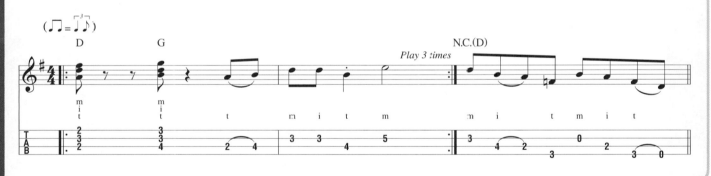

Miscellaneous: This week we're taking an open G major scale and playing it entirely with double stops of 3rds. Compare this with the scale form we used in Thursday's lesson from Week 3; you'll see how we're really just playing the same scale two notes at a time, with one starting on a different scale degree.

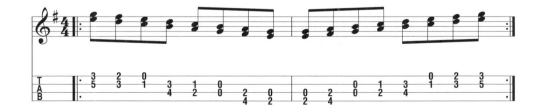

MON

Chord Vocabulary: Let's check out the closed forms for minor triads now. Since you should by now see how the process worked for the major triads, we'll look at both string groups (4–2 and 3–1) here.

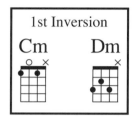
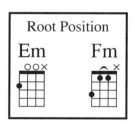
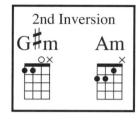

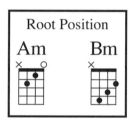
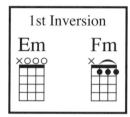
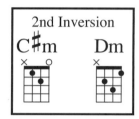

TUE

Strumming: In this exercise, we're alternating Bm and F♯ chords in two different forms: one on the 4–3–2 string set and the other on the 3–2–1 string set. With the strumming, we're playing straight 16th notes with alternate downstrokes and upstrokes, but we're accenting the upbeat throughout. Notice that the end of measures 2 and 4 also places an accent on the last 16th note (the "a" in the "2 e & a" count) of beat 2. For these accents, indicated with the > symbol, strum a little harder to make them stand out.

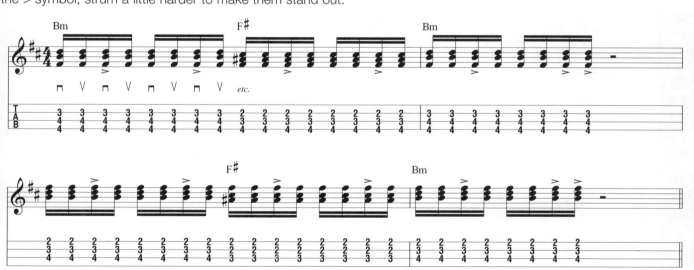

WED

Fingerstyle: Here's a rolling pattern using a few different root-position triad forms—Em on strings 4–2 and Bm and Am on strings 3–1—along with a B7 fragment thrown in for good measure. Notice that the plucking hand uses a one-finger-per-string assignment throughout. Regarding the fretting hand, I find that if I use my middle and ring fingers for the Am chord, it puts me in a nice position for the B7 chord that follows, as I can just replace my middle finger (fret 1, string 2) with my index finger (fret 1, string 4).

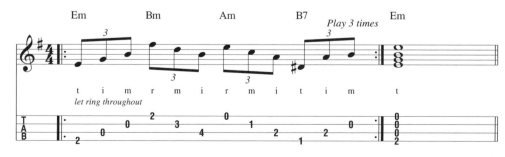

THU

Scale Exercise: We're using the same A Dorian mode as we did last week, but we've rearranged the notes so that we have three notes on each of the top two strings. This type of thing lends itself well to triplet playing, so that's what we've done here. I've included my preferred fret-hand fingering in the music, but there's room for other possibilities if you'd like. Regarding the plucking hand, I alternate the i and m fingers throughout here, starting with m.

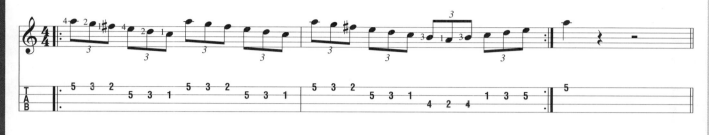

FRI

Legato: Yesterday's triplet exercise gets the legato treatment here. We're using almost all pull-offs, which is not easy—especially considering the fact that your index finger has to keep moving between frets 2 and 1. Take this one slowly at first and make your motions controlled and even. Your fret-hand fingers shouldn't be lifting way off the fretboard after you pull-off; they only need to be out of the way enough so that the strings can freely vibrate.

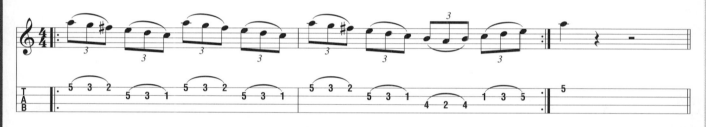

SAT

Licks & Riffs: Here's a very hip-sounding fingerstyle riff in Em that answers some quick descending arpeggios with a legato, bluesy bass riff. If you use your index finger for the final E note (fret 2, string 4), it will be easier to grab the D chord for the repeat because you can place the middle and ring fingers down first.

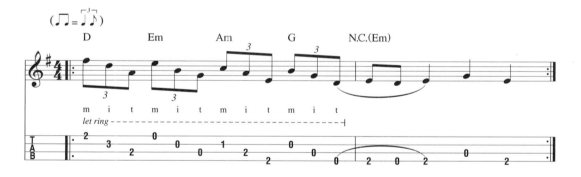

SUN

Miscellaneous: This is the same idea as last week, but we're using the C major scale instead of G major. The only difference between these two scales is the F, which is an F# in the key of G. Since we're playing double stops, however, that difference seems a bit more profound because we encounter the F twice as often: in the upper voice and the lower voice.

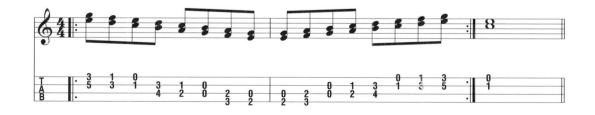

MON

Chord Vocabulary: This week we'll start tackling the open-voiced forms of major triads. We're going to look at all moveable forms from here on out. Obviously, if you move one of these moveable forms down to where one of the fretted notes is replaced with an open string, you have an open form, but the open/moveable forms don't apply as much to these voicings because they're going to span a lot of frets depending on the location (which strings) of the notes. So here are the three inversions of an F major triad in an open voicing.

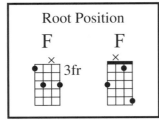

Root Position

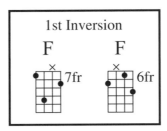

1st Inversion

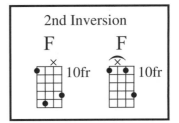

2nd Inversion

TUE

Strumming: Here's a funky example in F using two of our open-voiced forms from Monday: root position and first inversion. You'll need to mute the unplayed string within the chord forms with the finger above or below it (or both, preferably). For the purely muted strums (all X notes), just lay your fret-hand index finger lightly across the strings to deaden them. The strum pattern is a bit syncopated, so it's essential that you keep your strumming hand moving in steady 16th notes, only making contact when necessary (which is most of the time). Use your fret hand to sound the chords by pushing down at the appropriate times; your strumming hand just keeps on strumming.

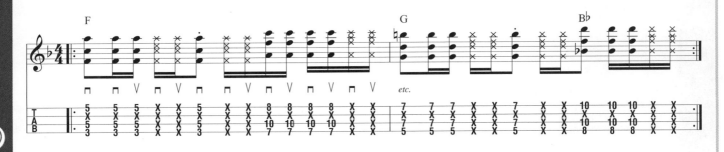

WED

Fingerstyle: In this E♭ riff, we see all three different inversion forms. Notice that the bass note is only plucked at the beginning of each chord (or sometimes preceding it by an eighth note). All of the triads use the 4–3–1 string set until the final measure, where we move to a 4–2–1 set. That said, I use a pluck-hand fingering of t–i–r through measure 3 and switch to t–m–r for measure 4.

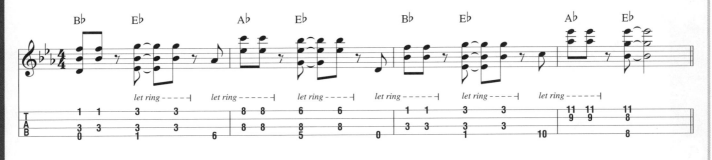

Scale Exercise: This week we have an ascending version of last week's exercise. Again using the A Dorian mode, we're starting low and moving up the scale with three notes per string. This also requires a constant shift back and forth with the index finger from fret 2 to fret 3, but it feels even more apparent because it's the first note played on the new string (instead of the last, as it was last week). Take it slowly and get the notes and shifts well under your fingers before speeding up.

Legato: And here's the legato version of yesterday's scale exercise. This one uses mostly hammer-ons, which are usually easier than pull-offs, but the shifting still adds a good bit of difficulty. Slow and steady is key in the beginning when you're first working it up.

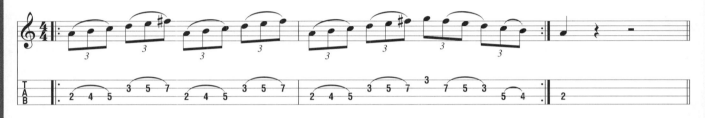

Licks & Riffs: Here's a pretty fingerstyle phrase using some open-voiced triad forms that are decorated with some melodic notes on string 1. For the second-inversion G chord, we climb up the notes of the G major pentatonic scale by way of hammer-ons and slides. Over the root-position D chord, we decorate with a hammer-on to the 3rd (F#) and a hammer-on to the sus4 (G).

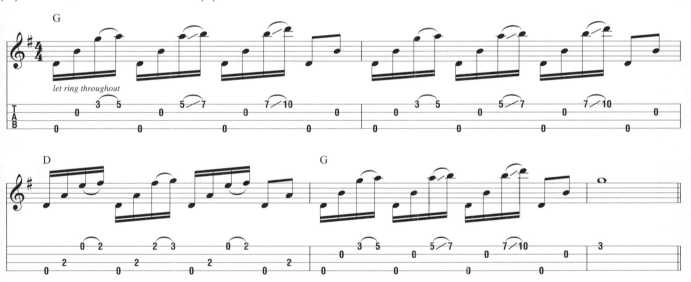

Miscellaneous: This week we'll look at a technique called **vibrato**, which is a repetitive fluctuation in pitch. There are a few ways to accomplish this on the uke, but one of the most common is lateral vibrato, which involves "tugging" on the string, as you hold a note, toward the bridge and the nut—back and forth. The closer you are to the middle of the string length, the more pronounced the vibrato will be. It's relatively easy to create vibrato at fret 12 using this method, but extremely difficult to do so on fret 1, for instance. I'll play the following line two ways: first without any vibrato and then again with it at the noted places (the squiggly line signifies vibrato) so you can hear the difference.

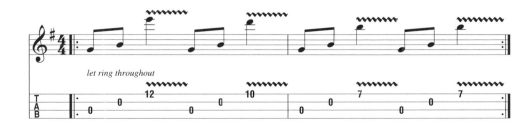

WEEK 31

Chord Vocabulary: This week we'll look at the minor versions of the open-voiced triads from last week. Again, we'll show these as Fm chords, and we'll have two voicings of each inversion. Although we don't have the space to work through them, you can take the same systematic approach with the other two types of triads as well: diminished (root, minor 3rd, diminished 5th) and augmented (root, major 3rd, augmented 5th). Although they're nowhere near as common as major and minor triads, it would certainly be time well spent with regard to your understanding of the fretboard and chordal theory in general.

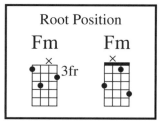
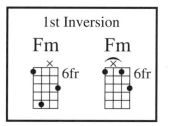
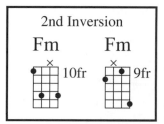

Strumming: Now let's incorporate some of these open-voiced minor forms into a strumming pattern. This is a highly syncopated pattern in which everything is an upstroke except for the first strum in measures 1 and 3. Again, be sure to mute the unused string in each chord by deadening it with the fingers on the neighboring strings.

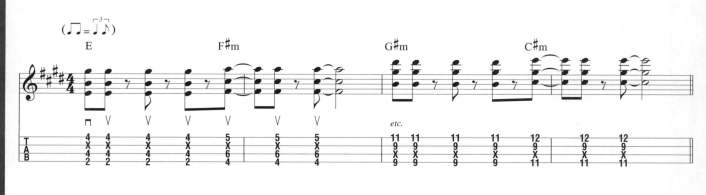

Fingerstyle: We've added our open-voiced minor triads to the mix here in a fingerstyle riff that's similar to last week. However, there's an extra element: the percussive "tick" technique that we first looked at in Week 9. The added challenge here is the fact that the chord forms switch between the 4–3–2 and 4–2–1 string sets, so you'll need to make sure you're actually plucking the right strings!

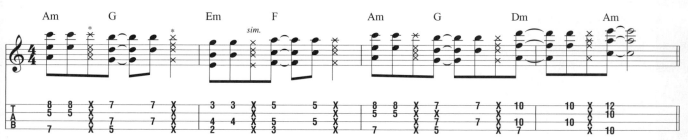

*Plant plucking fingers forcefully on strings to create percussive "tick."

THU

Scale Exercise: Here's a nifty little exercise using the A major scale in second position. After ascending straight up the scale, we descend by zigzagging in 3rd intervals. This entire example can and should be performed in a strict one-finger-per-fret manner in second position: index on fret 2, middle on fret 3, etc.

FRI

Legato: Now let's try yesterday's exercise with legato technique. You'll get lots of pinky practice on this one; the transition from beat 2 to beat 3 is especially challenging.

SAT

Licks & Riffs: Here's a jazzy lick that takes place over a I–VI–ii–V progression in D. The first two chords, D and B, are stated as open-voiced triads in a syncopated rhythm, and the rest of the chords are implied by a single-note line. After the B chord, shift up to third position and grab the A note at fret 5, string 1 with your ring finger. On beat 2 in measure 2, shift down into second position and remain there for the remainder of the lick. Notice that the pull-offs are placed on the upbeats throughout. This is a strategic move and helps the lick "swing," since it places a natural accent on the plucked note and de-emphasizes the downbeat notes—a common jazz phrasing device.

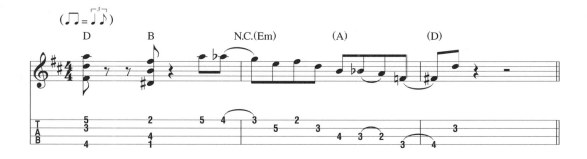

SUN

Miscellaneous: We'll get more practice with vibrato this week. This time we're applying it to chords. It's difficult to apply the vibrato to each note in the chord, so don't worry about trying to do that. You'll most likely only need it on the melody note, which is on string 1 in this case, to create the desired effect. The technique is the same as with a single note; play the chord and then tug on the strings repeatedly toward the bridge and then the nut, back and forth.

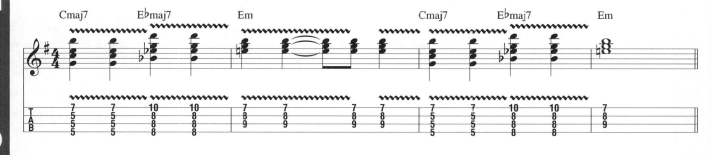

MON

Chord Vocabulary: We'll get back to exploring other chord types this week, and our next stop is the minor 11th chord. All 11th chords technically have six different notes—root, 3rd, 5th, 7th, 9th, and 11th—so we have to omit two notes to play them on the four-string uke. The root, 3rd, ♭7th, and 11th are considered essential to be a true m11 chord, so that's what we aim for. First up is an open Bm11, in which the root lies on string 2, and the moveable form shown as Cm11, which requires a full index-finger barre. F#m11 is next (root on string 1) and is demonstrated in moveable form with Gm11. Finally, an open Dm11, with the root on string 4, is shown in moveable form as Em11. In case you hadn't realized it already, all of these chords have been introduced as at least one other chord type when viewed with different roots. One of them is a 7sus4; can you determine the other?

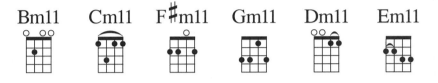

Bm11   Cm11   F#m11   Gm11   Dm11   Em11

TUE

Strumming: Here's a swung 16th groove that alternates m7 chords with m11 chords. Note that, even though there aren't very many strums going on here, your strumming hand should still be lightly moving in a double-time motion—i.e., down on every eighth note and up on every in-between 16th note. This is twice as fast as a pattern based on eighth notes (which generally tends to be at a faster tempo than this). If you keep your strum hand moving this way, the direction indications between the staves will line up perfectly.

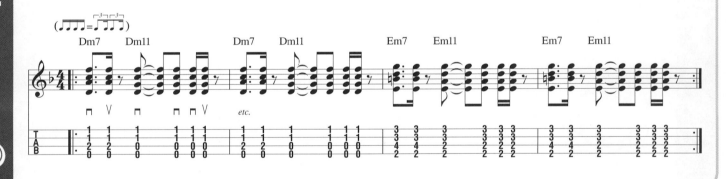

WED

Fingerstyle: Using different alternating m7 and m11 forms than Tuesday's exercise, we're creating a flowing fingerpicking pattern here in steady triplets that focuses on shifting string sets with the plucking hand. After first plucking t–i–m on strings 4–2, you shift over one string set to pluck strings 3–1 with the same t–i–m fingers. Be sure there are no hiccups in the tone or tempo when you shift over; start as slowly as necessary to ensure this. The result is a pleasant, undulating pattern that sounds great with numerous harmonies.

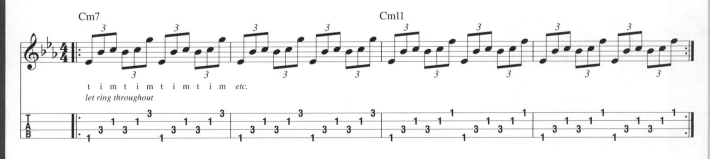

THU

Scale Exercise: This is the same idea as last week's exercise; we're ascending up the scale and then descending in a zigzag 3rds pattern. However, in order to include the lower strings here, we're using a new scale: E major. I've included my preferred fretting method in the music. If it doesn't feel right to you, feel free to experiment with other methods. Starting with your middle finger, the ascent isn't very problematic, with the only slight wrinkle being the shift up to second position on string 2. But when you come down, you have two 3rds in a row that lay on the same fret of strings 2 and 3: D#/B (fret 4) and C#/A (fret 2). As shown, I prefer to use two different fingers for the D#/B 3rd, but you could try rolling your ring finger if you'd like. As for the plucking hand, I'm strictly alternating m and i fingers here, starting with m.

FRI

Legato: And here's the same exercise as yesterday played legato. Again, the ascent isn't too problematic, although you'll get plenty of good pinky exercise. During the descent, though, you have an interesting event at the end of beat 3. Assuming you've rolled your index finger from string 2, fret 2 to string 3, fret 2, you'll need to hammer on to fret 4 with your pinky and then slide your index finger back to fret 1 for the pull-off that follows. This happens pretty quickly, but it's certainly doable with a little practice.

SAT

Licks & Riffs: Here's a nice, jazz-blues lick in G minor that makes use of a Gm11 chord followed by a phrase from the G blues scale in third position. I strum the Gm11 chord, play the descending blues lick with my i and m fingers, and then play measure 3 with my thumb. The tempo is slow enough here that you could play measure 3 with the i and m fingers using fingerstyle technique, but I like the sound I get from strumming it with my thumb. If you do choose to do this, however, you have to be wary of accidentally strumming the open B string, which will ruin the minor sound of this lick. To be sure I don't do this, I simply plant my i and m fingers on strings 2 and 1, respectively, while strumming with the thumb. Be sure to keep the fret-hand fingers arched in measure 3 so the open G string can ring out.

SUN

Miscellaneous: Let's look at another type of vibrato called **wrist vibrato**. This is the type of vibrato used by blues guitarists, and it can easily be transferred to the uke for when you're playing in a bluesy style. The motion comes from the wrist here. You hold the note and then rotate the wrist back and forth, similar to the motion of opening a door knob. You're essentially performing a bunch of quarter-step bends in a repeated fashion. On strings 4–2, you can pull the string down toward the floor and release it repeatedly to create the vibrato. On string 1, however, you have to change the motion or else you'll pull the string off the neck. So you'll need to push it up toward the ceiling and release it repeatedly to create the vibrato. Listen to the audio track to hear wrist vibrato being applied to each note in a G minor pentatonic scale.

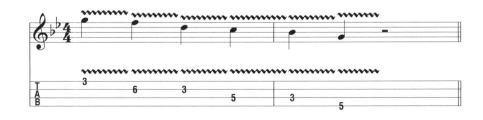

MON

Chord Vocabulary: Although major 11th chords technically exist, they're hardly ever used because the major 7th and major 3rd both clash with the 11th (same note as 4th). Therefore, the 11th is usually raised, creating a major 7#11 chord. Dominant 11th chords usually omit the 3rd as well, usually just replacing it with the 11th (or 4th). This essentially makes it the same as a 9sus4. So this week we'll move on to 13th chords, starting with dominant 13ths. The notes we'll try to include here are the root, 3rd, ♭7th, and 13th (same as the 6th an octave up). The first open E13 form places the root on string 1, and its moveable form (F13) requires a full index barre. The open B♭13 is a rootless voicing and includes the 9th instead of the root. For the moveable version (shown as C13), barre your middle finger for strings 2–3 and use the pinky for string 1. The open G13 is a nice-sounding chord (root on string 3) that requires a three-string barre with the index for the moveable version (A13).

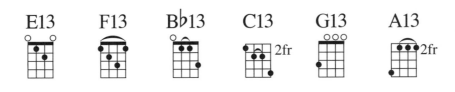

TUE

Strumming: This is a I–VI–ii–V turnaround progression in G that uses a rootless D13 for the V chord. Strum this with all downstrokes—I like to use my thumb—and keep them all short and staccato, accenting beats 2 and 4 throughout. The D13 chord is the only one that's sustained for a half note in measure 4, which helps to bring it out a bit. Notice that we're employing good voice-leading here for a smooth sound. We're using chord inversions so that the notes from chord to chord don't move much at all. If we had played each chord in root position—i.e., using a chord form with the root in the bass each time—it wouldn't sound nearly as smooth.

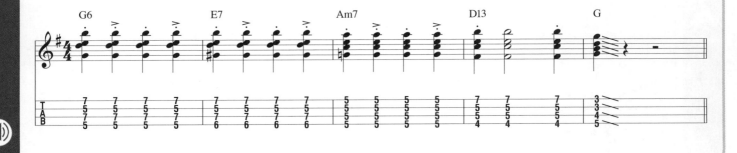

WED

Fingerstyle: And here's a I–vi–ii–V progression in the key of C played fingerstyle. (The vi chord in a jazz turnaround can be minor or dominant, depending on the song, though the dominant is more common.) We're using the open G13 form for the V chord. Regarding the fingerpicking, we're combining a few different approaches here to create a bit more variation, typical of what you might find in an actual performance. In other words, it's not so clinical. The plucking-hand fingerings are shown; we're sticking to one finger per string throughout.

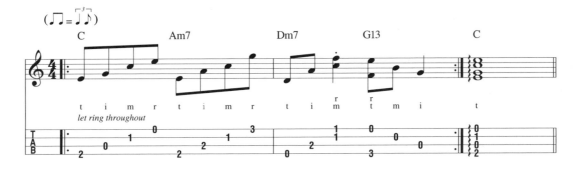

THU

Scale Exercise: This exercise is a bit of a handful, so be prepared. We're working with the E major scale again, but this time we're concentrating on shifting up the fretboard, remaining on strings 4–3 throughout. We play a two-beat sequence (eight 16th notes), shift up to the next position of the scale, play the two-beat sequence, shift up, etc. I've included the entire fret-hand fingering between the staves, as this one can get a little tricky. The shifts always occur on string 4 with your middle finger. Work this one up slowly at first to get all the notes under your fingers.

FRI

Legato: Here's yesterday's shifting exercise played with the legato technique. Use the exact same fret-hand fingering as you did before; the only difference is that you'll hammer or pull whenever possible. Notice also that we use a slide with the middle finger to shift positions each time. This is a *slurred* slide—not a plucked one. So in measure 1, for example, at the end of beat 2, play fret 2, string 4 with your middle finger, slide it up to fret 4, and then hammer-on to fret 6 with your pinky. This one is not easy, so don't rush it!

SAT

Licks & Riffs: This is a great jazzy lick that kicks off with an A13 chord played in a syncopated rhythm. The lick that follows is great practice for your pinky if you play it all in fifth position using one finger per fret.

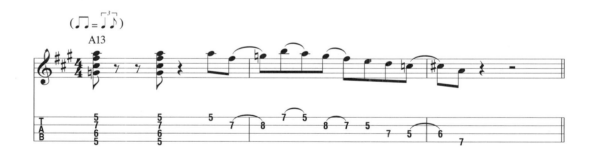

SUN

Miscellaneous: Now let's apply the wrist vibrato technique to a blues lick from G minor pentatonic. We're applying vibrato with our first finger (fret 3) and ring finger (fret 5).

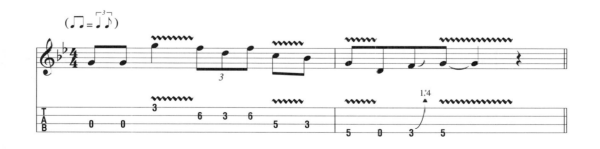

MON

Chord Vocabulary: We'll move on to the minor 13th chord this week. The first two open and moveable forms here—Em13/Fm13 and Bm13/Cm13—are simply the minor versions of last week's dominant chords. The only difference is that the 3rd has been lowered a half step. The final pair, however, is different, as it's not really possible to turn the last dominant 13th form from Week 33 into a m13. So Am13 is another rootless voicing that includes the 5th, ♭7th, ♭3rd, and 13th, low to high. The moveable form is shown as Bm13 in second position.

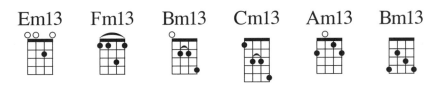

TUE

Strumming: Let's put the m13 chord into use here with a funky strumming pattern in A minor. This pattern mixes swung eighth notes with triplets and a good dose of syncopation, so listen to the audio if you're having trouble following the rhythm. I've included two different strumming options. Try both to see which feels better.

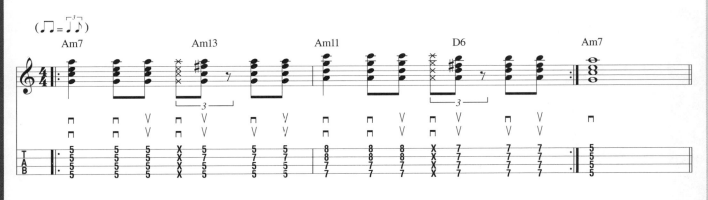

WED

Fingerstyle: Here's a mellow, slightly eerie-sounding pattern in A minor that alternates an Am13 with an Am chord. We're combining a swung-eighth alternating thumb pattern (measure 1) with a triplet alternating thumb pattern that we saw in Week 24. By simply alternating two different patterns like this, you can add an extra dimension to your fingerpicking arrangements.

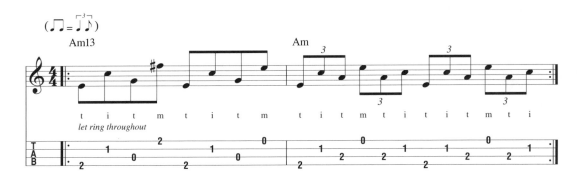

THU

Scale Exercise: This is a descending version of last Thursday's shifting exercise. We're still working the 4–3 string group using the E major scale, but we're starting up at the top with our pinky on fret 9, string 3 and working backwards. Again, the fret-hand fingering has been provided.

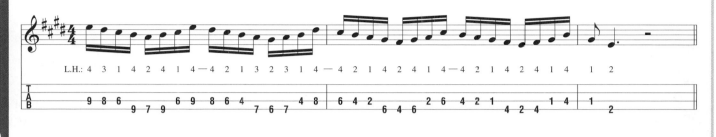

FRI

Legato: Here's the legato version of yesterday's exercise. The same idea applies here: you'll always shift down with the same finger—the pinky in this case—using a slide.

SAT

Licks & Riffs: Here's a burnin' little triplet lick using the E Dorian mode that climbs the neck to different scale positions while pulling off to a fretted note followed by an open string. Take it slowly and make sure that the notes are all clean and in time.

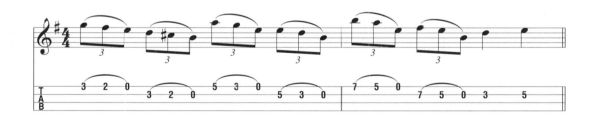

SUN

Miscellaneous: This week we'll look at another new technique called the **trill**. This is a rapid alteration between two pitches on the same string using hammer-ons and pull-offs. You can trill with an open string and a fretted note, or with two fretted notes. Any interval is possible (assuming you can reach), but half steps (one fret) and whole steps (two frets) are the most common trills. Each is shown here. Trills take a good bit of practice to work up, so don't get discouraged. Regarding the open-string trill, most players tend to use the same finger for trilling against an open string regardless of the interval; the index and middle finger are the most common.

MON

Chord Vocabulary: Major 13th chords are challenging on the uke, and there are really only two possible forms that contain the root. The first, Fmaj13, puts the root on string 4. The moveable version (Gmaj13) is a bit of a stretch but doable. The open Bmaj13 form (root on string 2) is not fun by any stretch of the imagination, but wait until you try the moveable version! Beyond that, we have to start omitting the major 7th in order to make the 13th playable. If we replace the 7th with the 9th, we'll get root, 3rd, 13th (6th), and 9th, which we call a 6/9 chord. It's a nice-sounding chord that's popular in jazz and rockabilly, particularly. The open Eb6/9 puts the root on string 4, while the open F6/9 puts the root on string 1. The F6/9 chord also contains no 3rd, instead substituting the 5th, so it's not technically a major 6/9 (it could also function as a minor 6/9). Neither one presents a challenge in their moveable forms. Notice that F6/9 could also be named G7sus4 and several other things as well. (Can you remember?)

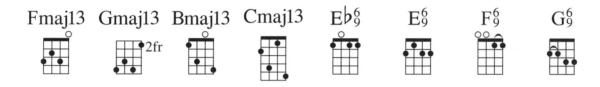

TUE

Strumming: The open Fmaj13 chord is put to work here in a 16th-note strumming extravaganza. We're strumming continuous, non-stop 16th notes using alternate downstrokes and upstrokes, but we're placing accents at strategic spots to create a groove. Start as slowly as needed to get a feel for the accents. If you're having trouble with the rhythm, listen to the audio first to get it down.

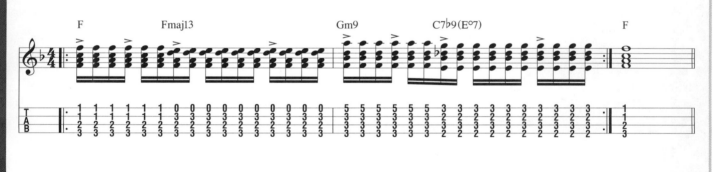

WED

Fingerstyle: In this exercise, we move from E6/9 to an Em13 (from last week) using a fleet triplet-based fingerpicking pattern that mixes in some swung eighth notes. We're using one finger per string on the plucking hand throughout, which shouldn't pose too many problems. The only real challenge here, aside from the mixing of rhythms, is that we're picking up the tempo a bit.

THU

Scale Exercise: This is another take on the scale exercise in Week 33, with a few changes. First of all, we've moved up an octave and are working on strings 2 and 1 now. Secondly, although we're still shifting up one scale position every two beats, the sequence is entirely different here. We're focusing on short bursts of speed (16th notes) followed by slower notes (eighth notes). The fret-hand fingering here will be the same as used for the scale positions in Week 33; we're just on strings 2–1 instead of 4–3. You'll shift every time with your middle finger on string 2.

FRI

Legato: This one is a pretty serious workout for the fret hand, so consider yourself warned! We're again working up through the scale positions of an E major scale on strings 2 and 1, but we're playing legato for a large percentage of the notes. You'll use the index finger to shift positions each time via a slide on string 2. Pay attention to the notes and tab because the pattern in each position changes slightly on the second beat to allow for the shift to occur.

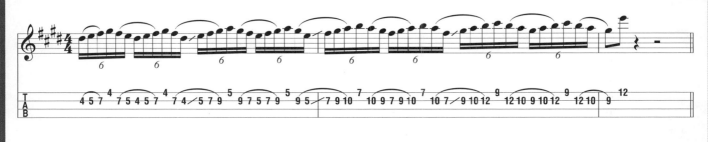

SAT

Licks & Riffs: Here we have a nice, little rockabilly-style lick that makes a great ending for a song in A. Aside from the opening slide from C to C♯—which I play with my middle finger—the entire lick can be handled with a one-finger-per-fret approach in fifth position. We bring it home at the end by sliding into an A6/9 chord from a half step below. Don't miss the staccato notes on beat 1, as they really help make this lick pop.

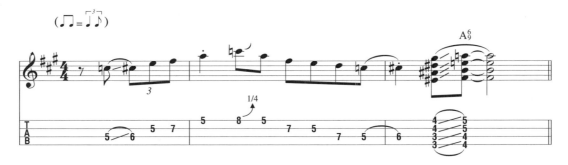

SUN

Miscellaneous: Let's take another look at the trill this week using a standard blues move in the guitar world. We're playing a double stop here at fret 5 on strings 3–2, which we're barring with the index finger. But we're using our middle finger to trill fret 6 (C♯) on string 3 to suggest an A7 sound. It takes a bit of practice to get down, but it's a great effect.

77

MON

Chord Vocabulary: We looked at a few major 6/9 chords last week, so here are a few minor 6/9 chords as well. The open Em6/9 and the moveable Fm6/9 are just the minor versions of the first two chords last week. The last two chords, Fm6/9 and Gm6/9, are exactly the same chords as last week. What? That's right. Since these chords don't contain a 3rd, they can be used as major or minor 6/9 chords.

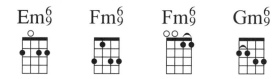

Em^6_9 Fm^6_9 Fm^6_9 Gm^6_9

TUE

Strumming: This is a smooth-sounding example in G minor that makes use of our new m6/9 chord. The Gm6/9 used here is the moveable version of the Em6/9 from Monday. There's a bit of syncopation in the strumming, but the real thing to watch out for is the decoration that happens at the transitions from measure 1 to 2 and from measure 3 to 4. Notice that the chord changes slightly (E on string 2 is replaced with D), and then a hammer-on at string 2 restores the chord as it was. A similar move is performed with the Cm13 chord. I use mostly all downstrokes with my thumb when strumming this. You can certainly alternate and use upstrokes for the upbeats if you'd like.

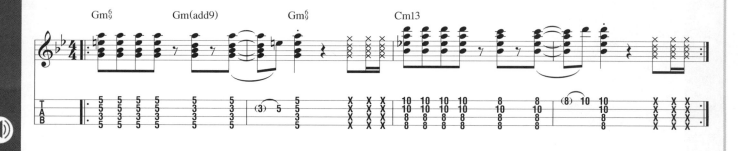

WED

Fingerstyle: This is an interesting-sounding pattern using our Fm6/9 chord along with some maj9 chords. On the plucking hand, we're using one finger per string and alternating a t/i–m–r pattern with t/r–m–i. To make things more interesting, we're syncopating all but the first chord (Fm6/9). Remember that, when moving from Fm6/9 to Gbmaj9, you don't need to fret the whole Gbmaj9 chord right away. All you need to do at first is barre the index finger across all strings at fret 4. Then you can take the next eighth note or so to fret the rest of the chord.

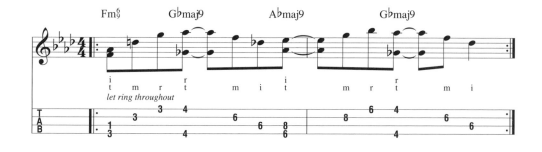

THU

Scale Exercise: Since we looked at the m6/9 chord this week, let's take a look at the scale that usually matches it: the **melodic minor**. This is just like a minor scale but with a natural 6th and 7th instead of flatted ones. We're using E melodic minor here, which is spelled E–F#–G–A–B–C#–D#, in second position with a 3rds sequence in ascending and descending form. At the top and bottom of the exercise, we've inserted a legato note so that the plucking hand can reset if you're alternating the i and m fingers. You'll want to start with the i finger when ascending and start with the m finger when descending.

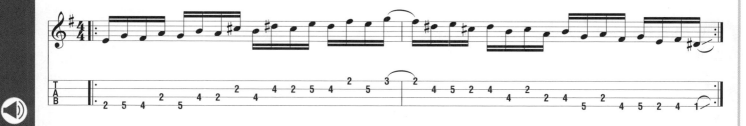

FRI

Legato: Here we're working with the E melodic minor scale exclusively on the E string, which allows us to take advantage of the open E note. In measure 1, we're ascending up the scale positions by hammering onto each three-note fragment following the open E. Coming down, we're doing the opposite: pulling off a three-note fragment followed by the open E. There are lots of whole steps in a row in this scale, so be sure to have your fingers in position before you step up the tempo.

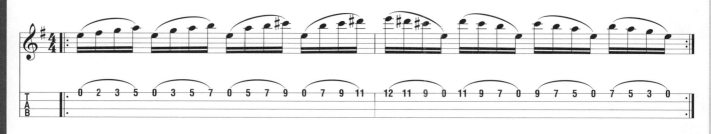

SAT

Licks & Riffs: Here's a jazz phrase in F minor using the F melodic minor scale in third position. This phrase can be handled for the most part with a one-finger-per-fret approach, with one exception: I prefer to use my middle finger for the C note at fret 5, string 3 on beat 3 of measure 1 rather than rolling my ring finger, but that's a personal preference.

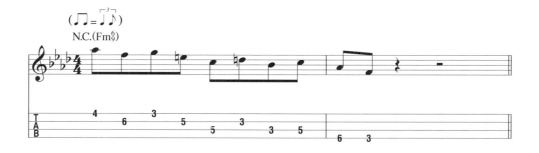

SUN

Miscellaneous: This week we'll check out another very expressive device: the **palm mute**. This is accomplished by lightly resting your plucking-hand palm on the strings at the saddle. This will prevent the string from fully ringing out and will produce a deadened, muted tone. The farther in you move (toward the neck) with your palm, the more muted and deadened the sound will be. Listen to the following phrase to hear how this technique sounds; the palm muting technique is indicated with "P.M." in the music. I'm plucking all of these notes with the thumb.

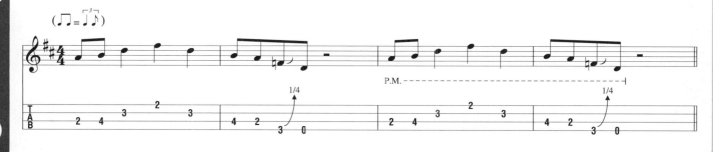

MON

Chord Vocabulary: It's time now to venture into the world of **altered dominant** chords. These are dominant 7th chords or extended dominant chords (9ths, 13ths, etc.), in which the 5th or one of the extensions has been altered (raised or lowered by a half step). They create a heightened sense of tension and are extremely common in jazz, among other styles. We'll look at the 7#5 chord this week. This is just like a 7th chord, but the 5th degree has been raised a half step. You may also hear this chord called an augmented 7th. Each of the three open forms (E7#5, G7#5, and B7#5) is presented as a moveable form as well. Compare these with the standard 7th chords to see and hear the difference. The E7#5 form puts the root on string 1, G7#5 puts the root on string 3, and B7#5 puts the root on string 2.

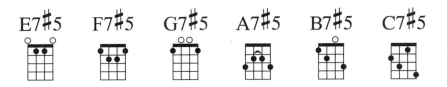

TUE

Strumming: Here's a I–VI–ii–V progression in F that makes use of a C7#5—a moveable version of the open E form—as the V chord. Pair downstrokes with downbeats and pay attention to the staccato markings.

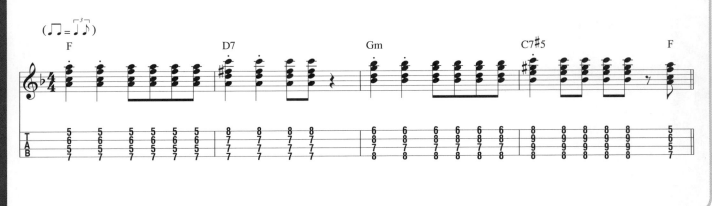

WED

Fingerstyle: Although altered dominant chords are by far ruled by the world of jazz, they can crop up in pop rock styles as well. Here's an E minor example in that vein that makes use of the open B7#5 form before resolving to a standard B7. The fingerpicking pattern is a simple up-and-down motion, but we've grouped the m and r fingers together throughout to provide a different texture.

THU

Scale Exercise: This one is a doozy. We're using a new kind of minor scale here: **harmonic minor**. This is like a minor scale with a raised 7th tone. The E harmonic minor scale is spelled E–F#–G–A–B–C–D#. The characteristic augmented 2nd interval (three half steps) between the b6th and 7th degrees lends this scale a unique and very recognizable sound. There are two major shifts you'll need to make here: one on beat 3 of measure 1 and another in beat 4. I've included the fret-hand fingering so there's nothing left to chance. Try isolating each shift—i.e., start a few notes before it and play through the shift—and repeating the section over and over at a slow tempo to build up your muscle memory before trying to increase the speed. Beat 4 is a real bear because, not only do you have to shift up an augmented 2nd (from C to D#, fret 8 to fret 11) with your pinky, but then you reach back to fret 7 for the B with your index, followed by one more reach up to fret 12 with your pinky. Needless to say, work this thing up slowly!

FRI

Legato: And here's another force to be reckoned with. We're using the E harmonic minor scale again, but we're in the higher octave in eighth/ninth position (and we shift to seventh position near the end). Not only do you have a lot of plucked notes falling on weak parts of the beat (and pull-offs occurring on the strong parts), but your fret hand has some serious work cut out for it. I've included my preferred fret-hand fingering, but you may want to tweak it a bit to suit your taste. Again, strive for an even flow of notes and try to naturally accent the downbeats as much as possible.

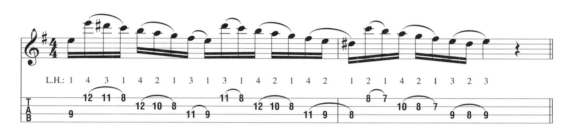

SAT

Licks & Riffs: Here's a jazzy line in A minor that makes use of the A harmonic minor scale in fifth/fourth position (see scale diagram). We begin with a roll of the plucking hand up an Am arpeggio. You don't want these notes to bleed together as when playing a chord. Therefore, you need to roll your index finger across strings 3–1 instead of barring it outright. Sometimes it's hard to get each note perfectly isolated, but you can get pretty close—close enough to where it's pretty negligible at this speed. Notice how we're implying the harmonies of the chords with our single notes: beats 1–2 contain notes from an Am chord (A–C–E), and beats 3–4 contain notes from an E7 chord (E–G#–B–D). This is a common concept in jazz; you can often hear the chord changes just by listening to the soloist alone.

A Harmonic Minor

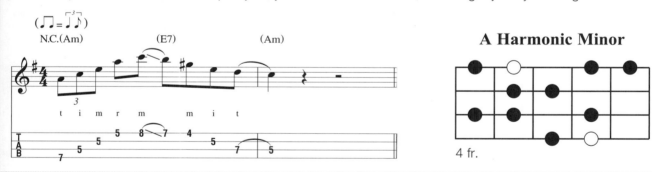

4 fr.

SUN

Miscellaneous: Let's put last week's palm-mute technique to work with a cool little riff that uses the open E minor pentatonic scale. Use the palm mute throughout here. For riffs that are slow like this one, I generally prefer to pluck all the notes with my thumb because I love the sound. It's such a great texture.

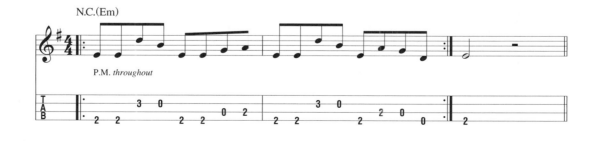

MON

Chord Vocabulary: Last week we checked out the 7♯5 chord, so this week we'll tackle the 7♭5 chord. This is a very interesting chord because it can be viewed one of two ways due to its construction. Depending on which note is considered the root, it can pull double duty as a 7♭5 chord that lies a **tritone** (three whole steps) away. All four notes are present in each chord, but they simply function differently. For example, D7♭5 is spelled D–F♯–A♭–C. If we look at the chord that lies a tritone away, A♭7♭5, it's spelled as such: A♭–C–D–G♭ (F♯). Bizarre, huh! We have two open forms here along with their moveable forms. Compare each one of these with their standard dominant 7th chords to see and hear the difference.

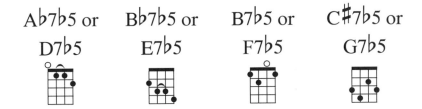

Ab7♭5 or D7♭5 | Bb7♭5 or E7♭5 | B7♭5 or F7♭5 | C♯7♭5 or G7♭5

TUE

Strumming: Let's put the new 7♭5 chord to work with a funky ii–V–I progression in G. After a root-position Am7 chord, we have the 7♭5 chord, which could be seen as D7♭5 or A♭7♭5, depending on how you look at it. To see it as a D dominant chord, compare it to the moveable 7th chord form from Monday in Week 11 (first frame). To see it as an A♭ dominant chord, compare it to the second chord from the same Monday's lesson. For the strumming hand, this is similar to the example we had in Week 30 in that we're mixing normal strums with muted ones throughout in a 16th note-based pattern. This one is even a bit more syncopated, so listen to the audio if you're having trouble figuring out the rhythm. Your strumming hand should be playing steady 16th notes (save for the very last eighth note of each measure); your fret hand dictates what is heard (chord or muted strum) and when.

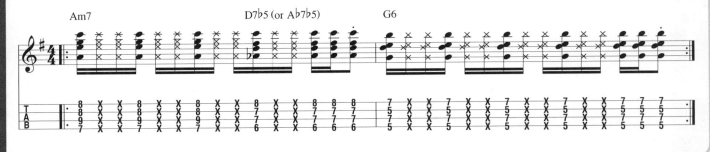

WED

Fingerstyle: This is a lovely fingerpicking pattern that gives the illusion of two different instruments playing. The thumb arpeggiates chords on strings 4–2 in quarter notes while the fingers play a stream of constant triplets on string 1 using a r-m-i pattern. This will likely take some time at first, so start slowly with the fingers only before bringing the thumb in. You should get that r-m-i repetitive pattern down pat on the open E string before trying the chords. Once you have the coordination down, fretting the chords isn't terribly difficult by comparison.

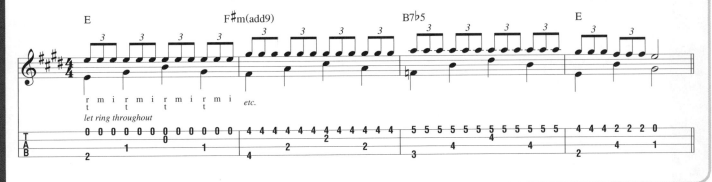

THU

Scale Exercise: Let's put our scale knowledge to the test here by stringing together four different scales that we've looked at thus far: major, minor, harmonic minor, and melodic minor. We'll play them all, in tandem, in the key of A using a zigzagging 3rds sequence. We'll try our best to base things off of first/second position here, but two of the scales (minor and melodic minor) will require a bit of a shift at the top of the form. This is a lot of notes to string together, so be sure you have each scale down on its own before you put them back to back. By now you should be getting pretty good at shifting, so I'll let you decide how you want to handle that aspect. I have, however, added my preference on a few of the more troublesome spots in measures 2 and 4. If you pluck this by alternating the i and m fingers, you'll find it's best to start measures 1 and 3 with the m finger and measures 2 and 4 with the i finger.

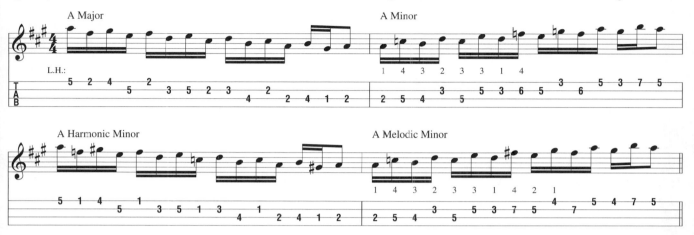

FRI

Legato: If you've gotten this far into the book and still have a weakness in your legato technique, this exercise will certainly reveal it. We have three pull-offs in a row on every string going down and then, after shifting up one fret, three hammer-ons in a row on every string. All four of your fingers are involved on every string, so there's no way to get around any one finger. You can continue shifting up one fret each time and repeat the exercise until you drive your cat to a frenzy.

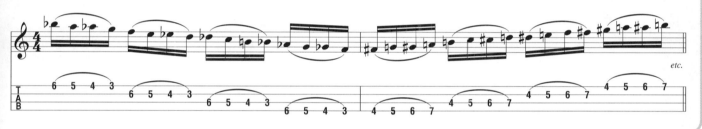

SAT

Licks & Riffs: I feel kind of bad for yesterday's lesson, so here's a sweet blues riff in E that gives you a good legato workout in open position. I use my thumb and fingers for beats 1–3 of measure 1, but after that, the plucking-hand fingering is pretty much whatever you'd like to use. The lick is a bit quick, but it's not terribly difficult. It just may require some time to build up the speed.

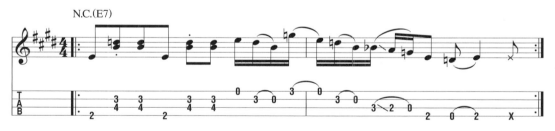

SUN

Miscellaneous: As another way to apologize for Friday, it's time to check out some blues turnarounds. Here's a classic turnaround in G that's guaranteed to put a smile on your face. It's a more fleshed out and sped up version of Sunday's example way back in Week 4. Another difference is that this one resolves to the V chord at the end instead of the I chord, which means this turnaround would be followed by another "chorus" (i.e., a 12-bar phrase) of blues.

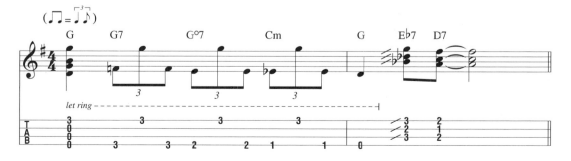

MON

Chord Vocabulary: We'll continue our altered dominant studies this week with the 7♭9 and 7♯9 chords. Compare these to a standard 9th chord to hear the difference. The first G7♭9 chord is a rootless chord and may look familiar. We talked about it briefly back in Week 18 when it was called a diminished 7th chord. The other open form, E♭7♭9, places the root on string 4. The moveable forms for both of these are very practical. E7♯9 is a rootless chord based on the open E9 voicing from Week 20, whereas the open E♭7♯9 chord (root on string 4) is the same as our open E♭7♭9, only the 9th has been raised by a half step instead of lowered. Again, the moveable forms for these are very usable.

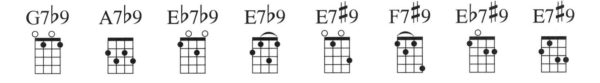

TUE

Strumming: Let's hear some 7♭9 chords in action. This I–VI–ii–V in A makes use of two of them, both in the rootless form, which is also known as a °7 chord: F♯7♭9 and E7♭9. Strumming-wise, there's nothing too new here. We've covered this pattern before, or at least something very similar, but the tempo has been jacked up a good bit here to give it a Western swing feel. Keep that strumming hand loose and moving on the beat.

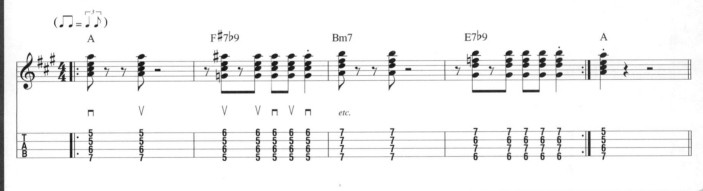

WED

Fingerstyle: Here's a pretty example in A minor that has a classical flair to it. Again, the fingerpicking pattern shouldn't pose too many problems, but the tempo is moving along at a decent clip here. We're making use of the open E7♭9 from Monday, alternating it with a standard E7 for increased tension.

THU

Scale Exercise: We've worked with zigzagging 3rds sequences a good bit throughout the book. If you continue that idea and move one more 3rd interval before you move down the scale to the next degree, you outline triad arpeggios. When done in a triplet rhythm, this makes an excellent exercise. We're working in the key of D major in second position throughout, playing a different descending triad arpeggio on each beat. I like to play this with a one-finger-per-fret approach, but that means being prepared for a few instances when you have to roll a finger over to the next string. Beat 4 of measure 1 and beats 3–4 of measure 2 require some thinking ahead by fretting with the pad of the index finger instead of the tip. This makes a stellar exercise for the plucking hand as well, whether you use i and m or just the thumb.

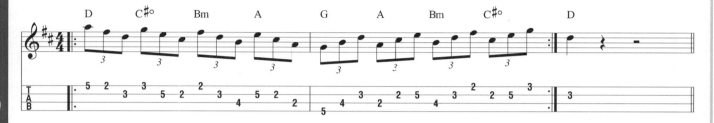

FRI

Legato: Here's a different way to play triad arpeggios that's a real barn-burner. We're using the same string set throughout (strings 2 and 1), with two notes on string 1 (the 5th and 3rd of the chord) and one note on string 2 (the root of the chord). Notice that we have two different shapes at work: one for a major chord (measure 1, D, and measure 4, G), and one for a minor chord (measure 2, Em, and measure 3, F#m). There's a little fret-hand stretching involved, but it's not bad. The main thing to watch out for is that you don't rush the hammer/pull move on string 1 that happens throughout. The lick will end up sounding lopsided and not nearly as impressive if you do. Work it up slowly at first to make sure the notes are even.

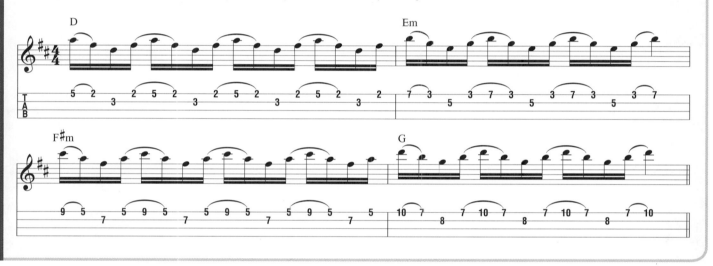

SAT

Licks & Riffs: Here's a classic example of using the 7#9 chord in a Jimi Hendrix-style riff. This one has a bit of everything: quarter-step bends, wrist vibrato, slides, and pull-offs.

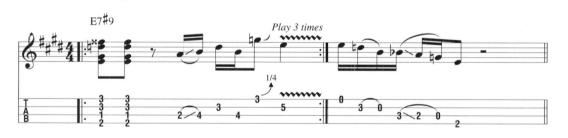

SUN

Miscellaneous: This turnaround in E is classic Delta blues style. The chord symbols shown are more implied than actually played. In other words, if you were to flesh out the chords instead of just playing two notes, that's what the harmonies would be.

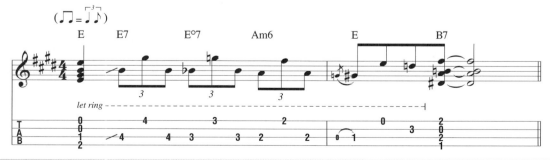

MON

Chord Vocabulary: We'll close out with some altered 13th chords: 13♭9 and 13♯9. We have three open forms for the 13♭9 chord—G13♭9 (rootless), E13♭9 (rootless), and B♭13♭9 (rootless)—each with a moveable form. But only one 13♯9 form is really practical, shown here as a rootless E13♯9 in open position and a moveable version of F13♯9. However, the rootless 13♯9 form shares the same tritone-substituting trait as the 7♭5 chord does, so each of these chords goes by another name as well, indicated by the chord symbols.

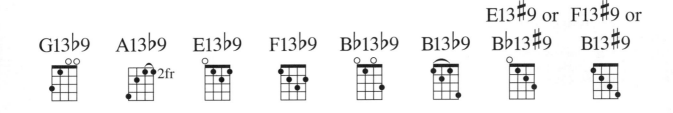

TUE

Strumming: Here's a rolling strum pattern in C that makes use of the open G13♭9 chord as the V chord. The pattern is a bit syncopated and mixes triplets and swung eighth notes. I've added my preferred strumming directions between the staves, but if another method feels better to you, feel free to alter it.

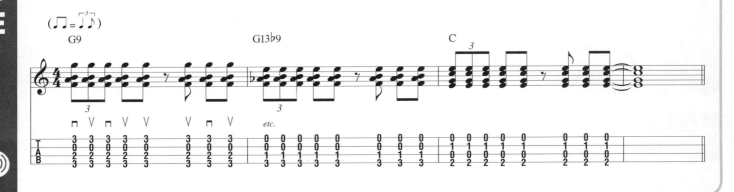

WED

Fingerstyle: This is a nice pattern that's reminiscent of a banjo. It's a little deceptive, so be sure to pay attention. Through the ii–V–I progression in G, we're repeating a three-note descending arpeggio with fingers r, m, and i on strings 1, 2, and 3, respectively. But we do this without stopping, which means the pattern starts on a different part of the beat each time. To help keep our place, our thumb plays on beats 1 and 3 throughout. At the end of measure 2, we pause the pattern at beat 4 and start it over again in measure 3 so that the melody can be properly aligned with the beat again. This independence between thumb and fingers will likely take a bit of time to work up, so don't be discouraged if it doesn't come quickly!

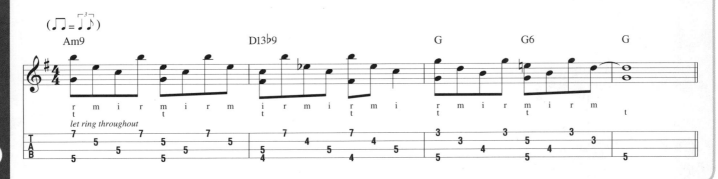

THU

Scale Exercise: We'll end with a monster shifting D major scale on strings 1 and 2. I've included the fret-hand fingering that I use; you'll be shifting on string 1 with your index finger each time.

FRI

Legato: This exercise is similar to Thursday's, but we've expanded the sequence in each scale position to two beats instead of one, and we're using legato throughout. Be very careful of the tempo here; when you combine shifting with plucking on weak beats, it can be very easy to stray. We're using the same scale positions as yesterday, so the fret-hand fingering should be apparent.

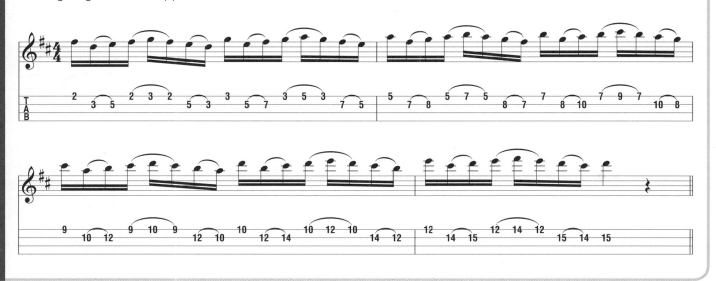

SAT

Licks & Riffs: Here we have a ii–V–I jazz lick in the key of C. After opening with a Dm7 chord and matching arpeggio on strings 1–3, which can be handled nicely in fifth position, we move into the G half-whole diminished scale: the matching scale for the G13♭9 chord. Built from alternating half steps and whole steps, it's an eight-note scale that's commonly used over this type of altered dominant chord. At the beginning of measure 2, shift back to grab the A♭ note (fret 4, string 1) with your index finger, execute the hammer-on to fret 6 and pull-off to fret 4, and then slide down to fret 3. The rest should fall into place from there.

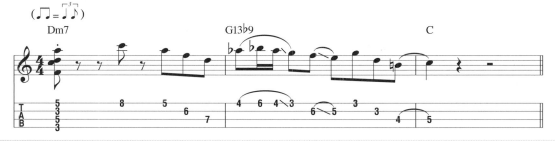

SUN

Miscellaneous: Well, we only have one more day left, but I have two really cool blues riffs to show you. So we'll do them both today. These are one-chord blues riffs in the style of Muddy Waters, and they can groove like no one's business. There's nothing terribly difficult here, but you really have to pay attention to the nuances—slides, staccato notes, grace-note hammer-ons, etc.—because that's where the groove lies. On these kinds of riffs, I like to strum with my thumb whenever I can because it really seems to get that warm tone that's so nice for blues stuff. Have fun with these!

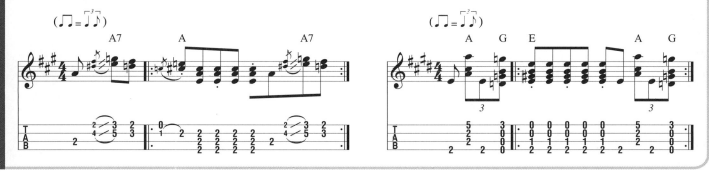

CONCLUSION

You did it! Congratulations on staying the course and following through. Sit back and take a breather; you've earned it. If you worked through this entire book, you've no doubt noticed a vast improvement in your technique, chord vocabulary, and lick repertoire. However, it's hardly time to rest on your laurels. Just as with any instrument, there's always something new to learn on the uke! Listen to other uke players—and players of other instruments too—for a never-ending source of inspiration; you'd be amazed at how many phrases from other instruments you can adapt to the uke. I truly hope you've enjoyed this musical journey, and I wish you nothing but success in your future endeavors.

ABOUT THE AUTHOR

Chad Johnson is a freelance author, editor, and musician. For Hal Leonard Corporation, he's authored over 70 instructional books covering a variety of instruments and topics, including *Ukulele Aerobics*, *Guitarist's Guide to Scales Over Chords*, *How to Record at Home on a Budget*, *The Hal Leonard Acoustic Guitar Method*, *Pentatonic Scales for Guitar: The Essential Guide*, *Radiohead Guitar Signature Licks*, *Teach Yourself to Play Bass Guitar*, *How to Build Guitar Chops*, *Play Like Eric Johnson*, and *Bass Fretboard Workbook*, to name but a few. He's a featured instructor on the DVD *200 Country Guitar Licks* (also published by Hal Leonard) and has toured and performed throughout the East Coast in various bands, sharing the stage with members of Lynyrd Skynyrd, the Allman Brothers Band, and others. He works as a session guitarist, composer/songwriter, and recording engineer when not authoring or editing and currently resides in Denton, TX (North Dallas) with his wife and two children. Feel free to contact him at chadjohnsonguitar@gmail.com with any questions or concerns and follow him at www.facebook.com/chadjohnsonguitar.